From Devon to Devonshire Vale
—The Milford Story—

George Milford

Copyright © George A Milford, 2019

First Published in 2019 by Harcourt Heritage & Tourist Centre Inc.

All rights reserved. Without limiting the rights under copyright reserved above, no part of this publication may be reproduced, stored in or introduced into a retrieval system, or transmitted, in any form or by any means (electronic, mechanical, photocopying, recording or otherwise), without the prior written permission of the copyright owner.

ISBN: 978-0-6486574-0-8

A catalogue record for this book is available from the National Library of Australia

Cover photo: Left to right: Ethel on the horse, Olive, Stanley, Ruby, Laura, Irene, Edgar, Leslie. On the ladder is Gladys Bailey, a visitor. Grandfather George was standing by the photographer.
Back cover: Edgar Milford.

Harcourt Heritage & Tourist Centre

Contents

The Milford Story: From Devon to Devonshire Vale	7
Where the furze brakes grow: Amos Milford	9
A Devon upbringing, 1820–1850	13
George Milford	14
A family migration	18
Safe home, safe home in port!	21
Building a home	22
Years of building	26
The community	26
Ploughing the land	29
John Kimber: A two-year visit to the New Zealand goldfields	32
Word from home	36
Tintype photo of Ann Milford	37
We blush to record	38
... that with dauntless breast the little tyrant of his fields withstood	42
Family matters: the boys provided for	46
A prune-coloured silk wedding dress	50
New Year's Day 1889	54
John Kimber moves to Castlemaine	56
John Henry Kimber	57
Money worries in the 1890s	59
Photographs	62

Up on the mountain	64
The land beyond goodbye	66
In the orchard	67
A dangerous business	69
Amos and Edith	72
Australian Natives Association	78
Death of George Milford	81
The governor's visit	83
Wartime conditions and thereafter	86
At Devonshire Vale: 8th August 1924 All the grandchildren	89
Appendix One The origin of the name Milford	95
Appendix Two Life expectancy in rural Devon	96
The Family Tree	98

The Milford Story: From Devon to Devonshire Vale

This is an attempt to tell the story of the Milford family. It has been compiled from reliable sources and tends to details rather than generalisations.

I recently visited a historic home furnished with pieces "typical of the period" but which were not the original items – the complete furnishings had been sold years ago. This was an unrewarding experience. By comparison, another historic home has the original furnishings of the family; sometimes chipped, sometimes of differing periods, but which, taken together, tell the particular family's story. It is this latter approach that I have taken. The story on the following pages is furnished with original information about the family.

Historians are warned that a wealth of detail may cause the reader to lose sight of the forest in contemplating the trees. Be assured that the detail has been chosen carefully. Much that is routine has been left out. I trust that the detail will illustrate, rather than obscure, the main theme, which is that our pioneer George Milford made the right choice when faced with the prospect of either walking in his father's footsteps as a life-long landless labourer or throwing in his lot with his wife's family on the other side of the world.

Recorded history often rests on the sensational, the criminal and the violent. Courtroom trials, inquests and political debates provide a solid diet for the historian.

There is none of that to be found in the following pages. As far as the Milford family is concerned, the well-known stanza from Gray's "Elegy" seems appropriate:

> Far from the madding crowd's ignoble strife,
> Their sober wishes never learn'd to stray,
> Along the cool sequestered vale of life
> They kept the noiseless tenor of their way.

However, this is a group of people who *did* live interesting and eventful lives.

It has been a pleasure putting this together. Here and there you may detect my father's voice. My father Les Milford was never a great storyteller. He only dealt in facts. Every so often, as we worked together on the orchard or in the cowyard, he would say, "My father did it this way", or once, while driving along Milford Lane he said, "That is where grandparents camped when they first arrived – they had to live in a tent."

But I will leave the last word to my mother. When I was about nine years old and resenting the fact that my name was not fashionable, I asked my parents, "Why did you call me George Amos?" Mum stopped in her tracks, drew herself to her full height and said, "Your grandfather Amos Milford was one of the finest men that ever lived."

This is the story of his environment and his origins. It is the history of our family.

Where the furze brakes grow: Amos Milford

The best place to begin our story is on the ridge of Great Haldon, "a pleasant walk" from Exeter, Devon, in South-West England. After leaving the hamlet of Dunchideock the road climbs steeply through trees until it reaches the top of the ridge and runs along it through gorse, pines, woodland and heathery moor. The height, about 250 metres, gives splendid views westwards of the edge of Dartmoor and, to the east, of Exeter and the Exe estuary.[1]

In the first decade of the 1800s Amos Milford came to Great Haldon ridge each year with the men of Tedburn St Mary. They came to cultivate and cut furze from the "furze brakes", to set fire to the bushes, then to cut and bundle up the very hard, partly-burned stems or "blacksticks" into faggots, (bundles tied with willow). The faggots were taken to Exeter to be sold as the very best fuel. Furze burns ferociously and gives a quick heat when put beneath a copper to heat water for washing, used to set a fire inside a bread oven or to revive a fire in the hearth.

So it was that Amos Milford, from the village of Tedburn, met and married Mary Whitburn, then employed at either Haldon House or Dunchideock House. They were married on 27th March

Furze gorse.

---
1   Muirhead, L Russell, Penguin Guides, Devon p. 62.

1813 in Dunchideock[2] St Michael's church, which has an intricately carved and beautifully restored wooden rood screen, a noteworthy series of carved roof bosses and carved bench ends ...

A population account taken 28th May 1821 shows that Amos Milford, labourer, and his wife Mary were then living at the tiny hamlet of Hembeer, about 1.6 kilometres north of the parish town of Tedburn St Mary. The household consisted of Amos and Mary and three young daughters. The only other residents of Hembeer were two other couples, each with children, and two apprentices. Of the 709 persons then living in the entire parish, 26 bore the Milford surname.[3] Between 1814 and 1833 Amos and Mary had a total of seven children, four girls and three boys. The fifth child, George, was baptised at Tedburn St Mary on 22 July 1827.[4] George kept this day as his birthday.[5]

Incidentally, there is no record of Amos Milford's baptism and we cannot identify his parents. At the time of his marriage he was said to be "of Tedburn St Mary". A clue to the local situation can be found in the transcript of the Parish Register of Tedburn St Mary held in the Devon County Record office which states "from 5/7/1778 to 30/1/1782 the entries for Tedburn St Mary are in a very illiterate hand and the spellings indifferent." Our search for background information and parentage for Amos Milford seems to be frustrated by a "very illiterate", and maybe neglectful, Parish Clerk.

Along with other children of the village, the Milford youngsters attended an elementary school. There were many schools in Devon towns and villages, supported by endowments, patrons,

---

2   Parish register, Dunchideock, Microfilm 4, marriages 1813–1836. Devon County Record Office.
3   www.cs.ncl.qc.uk/genuki/Dev
4   Parish Register, Tedburn St Mary, Year 1827.
5   Edith Symes' Birthday Book.

subscriptions or parish rates. Parish apprenticeship in rural areas took many children from school at the age of nine.[6]

Mary Milford died at Tedburn St Mary aged 46 years. She was buried on April 18th 1837.[7] Our ancestor George Milford, was not quite ten years of age when his mother died. The burden of bringing up the four younger children then fell on George's seventeen-year-old sister Sophia. Sophia did not marry until 1852.

At the 1851 census Amos Milford was living at Hole Rush near Hembeer. He was described as being 71 years of age, roadman on Turnpike Road. He was living with his daughter Sophia and son George. Hole Rush was a farm on the River Ted. Hole Rush is an isolated place about 500 metres from the church, and a further kilometer from the village along deep lanes. The homestead stood on a sizable farm of 30¾ acres. The farm was broken up into 16 fields, including about one acre of orchard, a half-acre potato plot, and a paddock with furze brakes (for fuel), with the rest in crop or pasture.[8] Each field was surrounded by a hedge, primarily of holly, hawthorn, blackberries and bracken; the hedges sheltered a lot of wildlife. This farm has been absorbed into a larger holding, the hedges have been cleared and the buildings demolished. Hembeer too, is not to be found, Upper Hembeer burnt to the ground and Lower Hembeer has gone to ruin in the woods. The Hole Rush homestead, sited where the River Ted crosses the lane between Lower Rubhay and Upper Rubhay, was on a slope above the rivulet which had a steep rise on the opposite bank.[9]

Amos Milford was employed as a roadman on the turnpike road. It was during Amos' lifetime that communications in rural Devon

---

6   Sellman, RR 1985, *Aspects of Devon History*, Devon Books, Exeter, p. 58.
7   Parish Register, Tedburn St Mary, 1836-1837.
8   Tithe list and map provided by Jean Wise, Tedburn St Mary.
9   Visited by Michael Vale and G A and J R Milford 28th August 2013.

were much improved by the development of the turnpike roads. Up to that time, remoter parts of the county seldom saw a wheeled vehicle and relied on packhorse trains for transport. Turnpike Trusts, empowered by an Act of Parliament, erected gates and took tolls for the improvement and upkeep of the road. It was only after 1815 that Macadam's method of surfacing made possible the full development of coaching. Macadam gave roads a cambered surface of small chipped stones, which, when rolled, compacted into a solid waterproof mass. A new road was pioneered from Tedburn St Mary to the outskirts of Exeter in 1823. This had easier gradients and avoided the narrow village streets. Regular passenger-coach services other than the Royal Mail then came into being. Improved roads and coaches broke down provincial isolation and made it possible for both mail and national newspapers to be rapidly delivered.[10]

Amos Milford, agricultural labour, age 76 years, died at Hole Rush, Tedburn St Mary on Good Friday, 21st March 1856; his cause of death was given as "Dropsy – 12 months". The death was registered by Sophia Vicary, daughter, Tedburn St Mary.[11] The men of the family had to go to the church to borrow a hand-drawn, four-wheeled bier to bring the body back for burial in the churchyard. The burial, delayed by Easter, took place on 29th March.

---

10 Sellman, RR 1985, *Aspects of Devon History*, Devon Books, Exeter, p. 41.
11 Certified copy of entry of death, General Register Office, England, courtesy Catherine Milford.

A Devon upbringing, 1820–1850

It was typical for children and teens, both boys and girls, born into a labourer's family in Devon to become an apprentice to a nearby yeoman farmer. The system of apprenticing children to husbandry was almost peculiar to Devon, or at least much more universal in Devon than in any other English county.

The Devon labourer enjoyed many advantages. He had an allotment of between half an acre and an acre on which he could grow potatoes and other vegetables, keep a pig and poultry and had cider, butter and scalded milk for the fetching.

A typical farm was some 250 acres in extent and the apprentices were of great value to the yeoman farmer. At first the children were set to fetching and milking the cows, driving bullocks to and from the fields, cleaning out their byres and bedding them down, digging, washing and boiling potatoes for the pigs, leading the horses or bullocks at the plough, with numbed fingers pulling turnips on the hillside field, and going out with the horse to gather furze to burn in the farmhouse kitchen.

Tedburn St Mary and nearby Crediton were famous as an apple-growing area. Every estate had an orchard and every farm, farmlet and cottage grew some apples.[12] The apples were mostly used for cider as the area was too far from major population centres for them to be sold as fresh fruit. Any young apprentice would have been familiar with planting, grafting, pruning, harvesting and juicing apples. The always predictable flowering, fruiting and harvesting was followed by cider making, the crowning event of the year. Days of hard work were enlivened by good company and good drink with promise of future contentment and joy.

---

12 Robin Stanes "*Old Farming Days, Life on the land in Devon & Cornwell*" quoted in *Here's to Thee Old Apple Tree* by Sandra Chalton, p. 12.

The yeoman farmer's family, along with the apprentices, got their meals together and could go to the bread and cheese whenever they liked. The apprentice boys all slept in the one bed. The children learned to read on winter nights and Sundays particularly. The farmer, if conscientious, had the apprentices say the catechism every Sunday and saw that they went to church. The children had their daily duties and rarely went home except at Christmas and Easter. Parents came to see their children whenever they liked. The young men who had been apprenticed did not marry before they were 27 or 30 and the young women not till a proper age.[13]

George Milford

George Milford married Sarah Ann Kimber on 13th July 1856 at the Register Office, Newton Abbot, Devon. He was 28 and his bride gave her age as 23 years. The marriage certificate describes George's "rank or profession" as Agricultural Labourer. Both bride and groom were residing at Bishopsteignton. There is an error on the marriage certificate which pulls back the curtain on this event. In the column headed "Father's Name and Surname" the Registrar has written that George's father was James Milford, deceased. It has been said that "agricultural labourers were known for using local dialect and people wrote down what they heard so it is more probable that the name was not pronounced how we would pronounce it today."[14] So, when George was asked to give his father's name he must have put the emphasis on the first syllable, saying <u>Am</u>-s, which the Registrar wrote down as "James". To realise this is almost to

---

13   Hoskins W G 1971, *Old Devon,* Essay entitled "The farm labourer through four centuries".
14   Waller, Ian H 1988, *My ancestor was an Agricultural Labourer,* p. 69

George Milford, about 1885.

Marriage certificate of George and Sarah Ann Milford.

16

eavesdrop on the proceedings of that summer's day in 1856.

Newton Abbot is important commercially as a road and railway junction and as the centre of a large agricultural district. Unlike the quieter towns of Devon it retains few old buildings. It is about six kilometres inland from Bishopsteignton on the Teign estuary.

Bishopsteignton is three kilometres from the seaside resort of Teignmouth and about twenty kilometres across country from Tedburn St Mary. We may assume that, after his father's death, George had gone to the riverside district looking for work or to visit relatives; there were families with the surname Milford listed at Bishopsteignton in the 1851 census.

In 1856 the immediate Kimber family at Bishopsteignton consisted of the widow Ann, described as a "Poulterer" (a dealer in poultry and game), elder daughter Jane (the wife of John Shilson) and younger daughter Ann (Sarah Ann, but always known as Ann). Their father Samuel, had died 8th September 1839 at the age of 45. Two of Ann's older brothers, John Kimber and Michael Kimber were then living in Victoria; John on a large acreage at Elphinstone and Michael at Muckleford. Their brother Charles West Kimber was then living in one of the suburbs of Exeter where he worked in a grocer's shop.

By exchange of letters full of advice and encouragement, John Kimber, well settled with his wife Charlotte on nearly seventy acres at north Elphinstone, had negotiated for the emigration of his siblings.

A family migration

John and Charlotte had sailed for Victoria on the ship *Bombay*, leaving Plymouth 29th August 1852 and landing at Melbourne 14th December 1852.[15] They had worked at "Stratford Lodge", Metcalfe for a time and then went to the Bendigo diggings. Having realised that the granite countryside around Mount Alexander bore a close resemblance to the Devon countryside,[16] John Kimber purchased land at North Elphinstone and carried on dairy farming.[17] Here they were joined by brother Michael.

Able-bodied men were in great demand in the colony of Victoria. Land and Emigration Commissioners in Britain selected people who would have skills useful to the new colony. These selected emigrants were granted a free or "assisted" passage to Victoria funded by the proceeds of the sale of "crown lands". John and Charlotte Kimber's voyage to the colony was under this arrangement. Michael's arrival in the colony is not recorded and it is family legend that he had been a seaman who requested to be paid off when he arrived at Port Melbourne.[18]

Soon after the Newton Abbott wedding of Ann and George Milford, final arrangements were made for Ann's older sister and her husband to join her brothers in Victoria. John and Jane Shilson sailed from Liverpool on 19th November 1856 on the ship *Herald of the Morning*.[19] They arrived at Port Melbourne on 1st March 1857. On landing at Melbourne they went to the Immigration Homes, a

---

15   State Library of Victoria, letter dated 9th October 1968
16   The country around Mount Alexander is, geologically, "Devonian".
17   Sutherland, A 1888. *Victoria and Its Metropolis*.
18   Information from Ida Milford. Michael's father-in-law was a ships captain.
19   A relic of this is a Holy Bible published by the British and Foreign Bible Society given "to John Shilson by his affectionate sister Mary Cox June 24th 1841", now in the author's possession.

long row of wooden buildings on St Kilda Road just beyond Princes Bridge, but left soon afterwards, giving their destination as Saw Pit Gully (Elphinstone).[20]

At Elphinstone, the new arrivals learned of their brothers' plans, for they were looking at land at the Faraday end of Harcourt, with a view to moving there. In 1858 the brothers completed the formalities for the purchase of two large blocks of land in the Harcourt–Faraday area,[21] while arrangements to bring out the fourth member of the family were coming to fruition.

Meanwhile, back in Devon, Ann and George Milford's first child had been born. Named Samuel, the child died as an infant.[22] It must have been with mixed emotions that Ann and George, at the behest of Ann's brother John, travelled to Plymouth to meet with J B Wilcocks, Shipping and Emigration Agent. In arranging for their assisted passage, the couple had to produce their marriage certificate, which the Agent duly endorsed with his office stamp as evidence that he had sighted it.

We may feel bemused by the fact that four of widow Ann Kimber's children chose to leave the family hearth to travel halfway around the world to start a new life, while Charles West Kimber had moved to the Exeter suburb of St Kerrian where he became a prosperous grocer.[23] This seemingly left their mother alone in the world. However Ann still had her extended family of brothers and sisters around her in her old age.[24]

---

20   State Library of Victoria, letter dated 11th November 1968.
21   Land Purchase of Allotments 37 & 38 of section 6, parish of Faraday dated 2nd November 1858 and of Allotment 2 of section 2 parish of Faraday dated 16th December 1858.
22   Per Death Certificate of George Milford, 30th April 1913.
23   Information from Pam Trickey, sent 6th June 1996.
24   Ann Kimber was buried at Bishopsteignton alongside members of the Foss and Taylor families. Her maiden name was Foss.

At that time, the southern counties of England were in a state of depression. Unemployment was high. The region suffered from the malaise of too few jobs and too many men. As a consequence, money was scarce and the labouring people were in the grip of poverty and the unrelenting twin evils of despair and frustration which confront the unemployed.

Ann and George Milford left Devonshire in the autumn of 1858 to travel to Liverpool where they were to board their ship for Melbourne.[25] At Birkenhead they were accommodated at the Emigrants Homes while the ship was being made ready. Imagine the feelings of the young couple, apprehension at the prospect of their first sea voyage, sizing up their fellow passengers, all strangers, choosing who to mess with, receiving advice and instructions from total strangers and anxiety over their luggage. At last the preliminaries were over and the ship sailed on 16th October 1858 carrying 391 assisted emigrants bound for Melbourne. [26]

The *Annie Wilson*, under Captain J Duckett, sailed by the so-called "Great Circle Route" to Melbourne. This took the ship far out into the Atlantic Ocean and so far south that icebergs, adrift from the Antarctic ice cap, were encountered. In those latitudes, the westerly winds sped the ship under full sail into Bass Strait, the first sight of land being Cape Otway, there having been no ports of call or even sight of land after leaving the British Isles two and a half months earlier.

---

25 Two keepsakes brought out by Ann Milford were a Holy Bible of 1848 "given by S. Brokenshaw to Ann Kimber 16th August 1851" and a tiny church Prayer Book with metal clasps given to Ann by Charles West Kimber.

26 Charlwood, D E 1983, *The Long Farewell,* Penguin Books, pp. 86, 87 & 160 publishes extracts of a diary written on the *Annie Wilson*. These extracts are very colourful and informative, but I do not think that the diarist was on the same voyage as the Milfords; the *Annie Wilson* made several voyages to Australia with emigrants.

Safe home, safe home in port![27]

On 10th January 1859, the *Annie Wilson* arrived at Melbourne, eighty-five days out from Liverpool, with the passengers all in good health and the ship reported as being "remarkably clean and well kept". Upon landing, Ann and George Milford were accommodated at the Immigrants' Home while a letter was sent to John Kimber advising him of their arrival. Whether a letter of instructions was sent back or whether one or other of John or Michael Kimber came to meet them we shall never know, the files of the Victorian Government Archives simply record the fact that Sarah Ann and George Milford left the Immigrants' Depot[28] on their own account for Castlemaine on 17th January 1859.[29]

After heaving their ship's trunk and carpet bags onto the Cobb and Co coach the newly-arrived travellers had to endure the lengthy journey from Melbourne to Castlemaine and then to travel a further hour to Harcourt. As darkness fell on that hot summer day, the four Kimber siblings were together for the first time in almost seven years, while George Milford met his brothers-in-law John and Michael Kimber for the first time.

They met on Allotment 1 of section 2A, parish of Faraday, land which had been bought as a speculation at the first land sales by J T Patterson, poundkeeper at Elphinstone.[30] J T Patterson had on-sold the land to John Shilson. The land, apparently unoccupied

---

27 Joseph the Hymnographer – the full verse is "Safe home, safe home in port! / Rent cordage, shatter'd deck, /Torn sails, provisions short, /And only not a wreck /But oh! the joy upon the shore, /to tell the voyage – perils o'er!"
28 The Immigrants' Depot offices were located in Spencer Street, between Little Collins and Collins Streets.
29 State Library of Victoria, letter dated 11th November 1968.
30 James, K and Davis, N 2008, *A History of Elphinstone*, pp. 97-99 and Crown Grants Register, Land Victoria.

virgin bush, had been surveyed and sold in 1858 by the colonial administration. Prior to 1858 it had been part of Dr William Barker's immense sheep run. What, or whose, land it had been before the arrival of the sheep was not a question that anyone bothered about. There were no Dja Dja Wurrung people in the district at the time Ann and George Milford came to Harcourt.

Ann and George's accommodation when they first arrived was a tent on the eastern bank of the creek, about sixty paces from the northern boundary of the allotment.[31] It must have been with a *frisson* of recognition the next morning when George surveyed the extent of the land and realised that it was exactly the same layout – a slope to the creek, a steep rise beyond– as he had known in his childhood home at Hole Rush in faraway Devon!

Building a home

George was enthusiastic to find himself on land which so closely resembled his birthplace. The Shilsons decided to turn over the land to Ann and George and to move to higher country about 500 metres away. They believed that the soil was better on the higher slopes. The views from the Shilson's new home block were of Mount Alexander, Mount Macedon and, to the west, Mount Tarrengowar.[32] In due course, John Shilson planted an orchard on the lower slopes and there was a well-worn path across Michael Kimber's land and along an unnamed road[33] between the homes of the two sisters, Ann and

---

31 A hawthorn tree, planted to mark the spot, survived until the drought of the 1980s.
32 The Victorian Minister for Mines visited Specimen Gully in October 1880 and was taken to this spot to "admire the picturesque view of wooded hill and clean dales, of farms and vineyards, which has few equals in the colony."
33 Now known as Kimber Road.

Jane. This was truly a family enclave. Michael Kimber routinely gave his address as "Devonshire Vale" at Harcourt.[34]

> I, the undersigned, hereby give notice that I have applied for a license for 20 acres of the land whereon this notice appears, under the 42nd Section of the amending land act, 1865, being part of allotment 8, secton 3 a, Parish of Faraday.
> MICHAEL KIMBER.
> Devonshire Vale. 623 16

George's first task was to turn over the soil in order to plant turnip seed in a large series of rows. Turnips grow rapidly in late summer and make a useful winter vegetable. In autumn, Ann and George got up before dawn to harvest the turnips into two buckets which George slung on a yoke to carry them, on foot, to Castlemaine for sale in the marketplace. This was their first cash crop. Soon they were making butter, also for sale[35]. In the winter they planted gooseberry bushes. In due course, these too bore a good quantity of fruit which was also sold in the Castlemaine Market.

An account of the Harcourt Fruit Industry published in 1907 says of the pioneers of the 1860s:

> "By dint of hard work, self-denial and perseverance, they gradually made ends meet and vehicles were purchased in which the fruit was conveyed to Castlemaine and other markets."[36]

George found that the soil he'd chosen for his vegetable garden was blackened to a great depth and produced a phenomenal yield.

---

34 *Mount Alexander Mail*, 16th June 1865, for example.
35 The butter mould design was a scotch thistle. The butter mould was sold in 1972.
36 *Mount Alexander Mail*, 15th August 1907 – "Harcourt Fruit".

Unbeknown to the new settlers, the land had been a camping spot for the indigenous inhabitants for hundreds of generations, and the blackened soil was the site of a midden, the accumulation of thousands of years of Dja Dja Wurrung occupation.

As a matter of urgency, the men proceeded to build a cob house. Cob houses are only to be found in Britain in Devon, Somerset and south Wiltshire.[37] Using a mixture of clay, small stones, straw and water, the walls were built on a stone foundation. The mixture was well pounded in a tub and then laid on, course by course, while still wet. No formwork was used. The faces of the wall were pared down with a spade as the work progressed. A course of cob could only be laid to a depth of about 18 inches, otherwise the material would tend to bulge. A course would be covered and allowed to harden for some days before another course was laid down. The walls were about 15 inches thick and the corners were rounded to reduce the likelihood of cracking. When finished, the wall was plastered inside, and the outside was weatherproofed with successive coats of lime wash. This unique building, with its distinctly rounded corners, still stands 160 years later. There was urgency about this building project because Ann was pregnant.

Michael Kimber Milford was born on 29th November 1859 at Harcourt. Dr W F Preshaw, the district's senior medical man was present at the birth. Unfortunately the child did not do well. Despite Dr Preshaw's attendance, the baby died on the 23rd January 1860. The child's cause of death was given as "dysentery, ill since birth". He was buried at Castlemaine Cemetery on 26th January. His death certificate gives the name of George Milford as the undertaker.[38]

---

37 Henderson, AS 1964, *The Family House in England*, Littlehampton Book Services Ltd, p. 87.
Miles, L 1977, *Victorian Primitive,* Greenhouse Publications, p. 39.

38 Noted in birth and death certificates for Michael Kimber Milford.

Regrettably, on 5th February 1862 George had to perform the same sad duty for his three-month old son William.[39] On the whole, infant deaths were in the majority in the early years of settlement and, for January 1860, comprised two thirds (64/95) of all deaths in the Castlemaine district.[40]

Michael Kimber married Ellen Freher on 2nd February 1862 at St Mary's Church, Castlemaine. The marriage was performed by the Revd. Father Pat Smyth.[41] Michael, a farmer, was 28 years old and Ellen, who had been born in Co Tipperary, was 22. She was described as a servant, of Barkers Creek.

On 28th September 1862 Ann gave birth, at home, to a baby girl, Jane.[42] This child grew and thrived. Four more boys were born to Ann and George over the next nine years while Ellen and Michael Kimber had ten children in the years 1863 to 1879. Ann and George's youngest child, George Amos Milford, was born at Harcourt 6th September 1876.

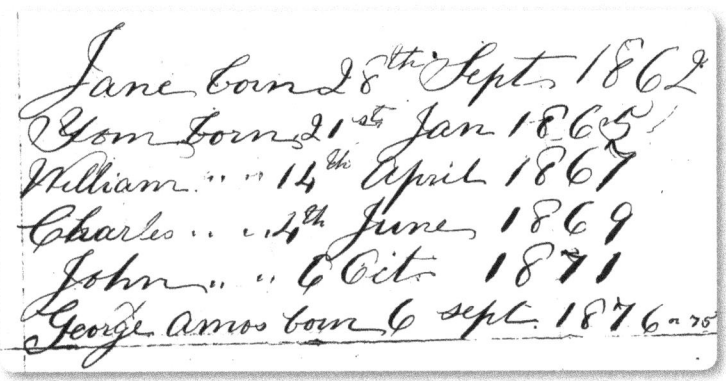

Written by George Milford.

---

39 Michael was buried in C of E grave 114 and William in C of E grave 365.
40 *Mount Alexander Mail*, 8th February 1860.
41 Father Smyth was the priest who saved the life of Peter Lalor after the storming of the Eureka Stockade.
42 Known as Jane Kimber Milford, later Jane K Frost.

Years of building

As the family expanded and the children grew, the home was extended. During the 1870s a brick house was built adjacent to the cob house, and a weatherboard kitchen was added. A timber apple-house with stables was built to the north of the house. This complex became the homestead of a large land holding.

By selection and purchase, George added to his land holdings eventually planting about 42 acres of orchard on his total acreage of about 130.

Allotment 1 section 2A 20a2r11p
Allotment 6 section 5A 19a2r20p
Allotment 7 section 5A 22a3r33p
Allotment 33 section 4 36a2r16p
Allotment 34 section 4 30a1r13p

making a total of 130acres 0roods 13perches.

This was a good achievement for one who arrived in the Colony as a landless Agricultural Labourer. George's accumulation of land was similar to that of his brothers-in-law, so that the extended family had a considerable swathe of land, some under orchard, in the valley that they knew as "Devonshire Vale".

The community

Beyond the family enclave, the Harcourt community was growing. Other than relatives, Ann and George's nearest neighbours, were John Foster and John Slaven to the east, the Lang family to the south, and Anna and William Schier to the north. Communication between the German Schiers, the Devon folk and the Scottish Langs, each with their distinctive accent, must have been difficult.

The fact that Harcourt soils were not gold-bearing meant that settlement was sparse and slow to grow. Doctor William Barker, who had arrived in 1845, was the local squatter. Dr Barker, who had extensive landholdings and was a friend of Governor la Trobe, was a bachelor who left the district and abandoned sheep herding to return to medical practice in 1862.

There were three hotels in Harcourt – the Harcourt Hotel, the Live and Let Live and the Talbot Inn. The Harcourt Hotel also did duty as the post office. A primary school opened in late 1859. There was no resident medical doctor, except during the construction of the railway (and he was a drunkard). The Wesleyans and the Bible Christians each had a foothold in the Barkers Creek, Faraday and Harcourt communities, and the Rechabites opened a tent in the late 1860s.[43]

A congenial young man named Samuel Sutton had, in 1853, been the first to prove the suitability of the soil for horticulture. Samuel Sutton, who hailed from Warwickshire, was an advocate of soil trenching to establish the fruit trees. Nathaniel Vick, Henry Ely and William Eagle had planted apple orchards and led the way for many others to follow.

There was no regular supply of water in the district, apart from the creeks and springs, so watering of newly planted apple trees became a task for bucket and a sled-mounted barrel. The original rootstocks came from Whatmough's orchard nursery at Greensborough. Later in the century, Lang's "Talbot Nursery" supplied rootstock and seeds. Charles Thacker planted a commercial vineyard. Dairying was a low-threshold way of using the land with "farmers' commons" available to graze cows and horses on public land for a small annual fee. A granite quarry had been opened up on Mount Alexander and,

---

43 The Plymouth Brethren arrived later in the century with the Eagle family and Henry Robert Bastow.

at first, provided only spasmodic work to skilled masons having a spell from the Forest Creek diggings.

There had been a considerable population at nearby Barkers Creek during the gold-rushes of 1851 and in later years but the poorer soil of the goldfields meant that the gold diggings were at the start of a long, steady decline at the time that Harcourt folk were clearing their lands to establish dairies and apple orchards. A floating population of labourers, stonemasons and camp-followers was a feature of the district between 1859 and 1862 during the construction of the Melbourne to Murray River railway. Another boost to the local population took place during the construction of the Barkers Creek Reservoir in 1867. There was no police station at Harcourt except during these two temporary periods of population growth. These big construction projects also provided temporary work for the local farmers. The contractors advertised for "pick and shovel men" and offered good day rates for men who could bring a horse and dray to the worksite. Local government, which was busy constructing roads and bridges, was centred at far-off Metcalfe.

The local "movers and shakers" were Irish-born men – gregarious, talkative and prone to formulating petitions to the Shire Council or submitting "memorials" to the colony's government. This group met at Slattery's Harcourt Hotel and took its lead from the schoolmaster, Henry Hayden, who held a Bachelor of Arts degree from Trinity College, Dublin. It was through the efforts of this group that the school had been opened, a cemetery established and charity fundraising took place. The Milford-Kimber families took no part in this except to sign the occasional petition. Their lack of involvement was probably due to the distance of their holdings from the village centre and also the all-consuming demands of making a living.

The market town was Castlemaine, and the local newspaper

was the *Mount Alexander Mail*. Given that Castlemaine, with all of its amenities, was an hour's drive from Harcourt, the European pioneers of the lands at the foot of Mount Alexander would have been inclined to agree with the terse comment of Edward O'Keefe, reservoir construction contractor, that Harcourt was "a wild and remote place".

Ploughing the land

In this uncultivated wilderness, the first task of the pioneers, after felling and burning the native timber was to plough their acreage. This work was done using a single-furrow plough. An observer of early settlement[44] wrote:

> "In the early years after clearing the land the plough continued to go around the obstinate blackened log or deep-rooted stump. Many a time a hidden root sent the holder of the single-furrow plough spinning from his furrow."

The undulating terrain of the country around Mount Alexander presented as good tillable land. It was hilly country, but the heights and gradients were no deterrent to cultivation. Back home in Devon, they and their forebears, had ploughed up everything there was to plough, even quite steep land, a fact that so impressed Lord Protector Oliver Cromwell in 1645 and 1646 that he asserted: "I have visited all the counties of England and the Devonshire husbandry is the best." Later writers made similar remarks.[45]

---
44 Fullerton, Mary Eliza 1921, *Bark House Days*.
45 Stanes, Robin 2009, *The husbandry of Devon and Cornwall,* pp. 3-10.

The hillsides on the west of the Kimber and Milford holdings were so steep that a horse could not keep its footing. Two horses were harnessed to the plough, the upper horse having to pull upwards as well as forward to overcome gravity and keep the single-furrow plough at its work. The plough turned the furrows downhill, over the years creating "lands" at least a metre in height, so that part of the orchard was on "steps", making it difficult, at harvest time, to pick fruit from the lower side of the trees planted uniformly across the hillside.

It is probable that the slope from Faraday Road to the creek was the first to be planted in fruit trees. It was the custom to trench the soil to at least two spades depth. The trench had to be cut through the sandy loam topsoil and the white sandy subsoil into the clay. The clay was mixed with the sandy soils when the trench was re-filled. This gave the tree roots a sure grounding, which helped them to survive the dry summers. This trenching was a huge task for the first settlers. After planting, seven years would pass before the trees came into fruit.

Ann and George Milford were extremely fortunate in the timing of their arrival and establishment. They were able to set out and plant an orchard before an irrigation system was available. This was possible because, during the first ten years in which they brought the orchard into full bearing, the average annual rainfall was 595 mm (1862-1872), with only one year when rainfall was less than 300mm. These rainfall figures have not been achieved in the 21st century, so that Harcourt orchardists now rely heavily on the Malmsbury and other Coliban River storages. The creek, a tributary of Black Jack Creek, which in turn is a tributary of Barkers Creek, was fed by springs that rose further up the gully in Lang's hundred acre property. This creek was quite reliable; it has since been impeded by dams built by the Lang family. The water situation has changed considerably in the 160 years that have passed since Ann and George arrived. Given today's climate and conditions our pioneers might have thrown in the towel altogether.

Fence-to-fence ploughing was an annual task from the outset. Nearer to Harcourt, neighbor William Schier was also busy with the plough, the local newspaper reporting on the well-cultivated garden of Mr. Schier:[46]

> "... the soil where the fruit trees are growing is of a dark loamy nature intermixed with rough sand, but it appears to be suitable for fruit-growing purposes. It is ploughed first and afterwards harrowed when the weeds are extirpated. The garden is free from these, which shows great attention is paid to it by its owner."

Harcourt's sandy soils, when damp, lend themselves to the use of the spring-tined harrow, an American invention patented in 1869. It was really a light cultivator with backwards curving tines so tensioned by the frame that they would spring back into position after they encountered any obstruction in the soil. These harrows sat flat upon the ground; engaging them to achieve the right depth of cultivation was effected by a lever/ratchet. Two horses were needed for these harrows. With the need for horses came the need for fences, and stabling, and land to grow hay for chaff. The pioneers accumulated a large amount of working equipment. The extent of one man's holdings is shown in the next chapter.

---

46 Ormond, Judy and E.N. Maree Hogan 1982, *The Schier family, 1812-1982*.

John Kimber: A two-year visit to the New Zealand goldfields

John Kimber had "gold fever". He had first contracted the condition on the Bendigo diggings in the mid-1850s. John had been able to find sufficient gold in the Bendigo creek to enable him to purchase a big acreage, back on the granite country, at North Elphinstone, which he stocked with dairy cattle to supply milk, cream and butter.

In the early 1860s the *Mount Alexander Mail* provided comprehensive reports of the New Zealand goldfields. On May 9th 1862 the *Mail*[47] gave a description of the diggings at Gabriel's Gully (the Tuapeka) –

> "A narrow winding ravine about three miles in length deeply sunk between treeless grassy ranges. The bed of the valley torn up, as only diggers can tear up the soil. Nearly all the tents are of calico. The cold rains of the summer seemed to create a general dread of the promised rigours of winter. The Blue Mountains which constitute the western boundary of the horizon at Tuapeka, were visibly covered by snow. The workings in Gabriel's Gully are six to sixteen feet in depth. The wash dirt is rarely more than a few inches thick. Every man spoken to acknowledged that he was getting gold. Nuggets are rare, coarse gold is less plentiful than fine."

Family ties were strong, but the lure of gold was stronger. John Kimber was determined to go to the gold diggings of the Otago. A later report, written during winter, was fully printed in the *Mount*

---

47 *Mount Alexander Mail*, 9th May 1862.

Alexander Mail on September 8th 1862[48]. It cautions would-be miners and reminds its readers:

> "… it is well-known that a large proportion of those who go from Victoria have not the least idea of making Otago their home. The climate, after our glorious Victorian atmosphere, is abominable. Settlement is in its infancy, the comforts and luxuries that we have now attained are, and must be, for many years, unknown.
>
> "Our soil is unsurpassed in the world and visions of vines, fruits and flowers of all kinds, will constantly recur to the Victorian emigrant and he will not be able to avoid comparison there with the snow, the sleet and the cheerless winters of New Zealand. The New Zealand gold will purchase Victorian farms and the labours of Victorians will prove equally advantageous to both colonies".

This was food for thought and would have been much discussed between John, his siblings and in-laws, some of whom were avid readers of the *Mail*. The phrase *"New Zealand gold will purchase Victorian farms"* clinched the argument for John Kimber. Alluvial gold won at the Bendigo diggings had given him a step up the economic ladder and he intended that New Zealand gold would do the same on a larger scale.

Later reports from New Zealand indicated that there were rushes to the Arrow River and the Shotover followed by more rushes. John

---

48 *Mount Alexander Mail*, 8th September 1862.

Kimber placed his affairs in the hands of T. W. Adams, auctioneer, and in due course the advertisement shown below appeared in the *Mail*.[49]

> **Freehold Farms, Property, &c.,**
> AT
> NORTH ELPHINSTONE & FARADAY.
>
> MR. T. W. ADAMS has instructions from Mr. JOHN KIMBER, to sell by public Auction, on the premises, at North Elphinstone,
>
> **On Tuesday, the 10th February,**
> At 11 o'clock punctually, all that Valuable
>
> **Allotment of Land !!**
>
> Situate at North Elphinstone, containing 3 Acres, more or less, and being lots 165, 166, and 167, of portions 14C and 14D of subdivision of Section 2, all closed fenced and under cultivation, with buildings thereon erected. Also part of portion 26 of Section 1, situate in the parish of Elphinstone, containing 15a. 3r. 33½p., partly fenced. Also allotments No. 37 and 38 of Section 6, parish of Faraday, containing 50 acres, all substantially fenced, partly under cultivation. A good supply of water all the year round.
>
> Titles to the Land guaranteed. For further particulars apply to the auctioneer.
>
> **48 Head ᵒᶠ mixed Cattle**
> In good condition, consisting of
> Milch Cows
> Steers
> Yearlings, &c.
> Horse, spring cart, and harness,
> Draught mare, cart and harness.
> Farming implements
> Household Furniture
> Pigs, Poultry, &c.
> NO RESERVE.   TERMS CASH.
> 463 feb 10

The advertisement shows that John and Charlotte Kimber were gambling everything on success in New Zealand. The advertisement gives an insight into the workings and equipage of the farm. It also

---

49   *Mount Alexander Mail*, 2nd February 1863.

shows the extent to which they had prospered since landing at Melbourne as immigrants just ten years earlier.

John and Charlotte sailed out of Melbourne for Otago, NZ on the ship *Eli Whitney* in March 1863[50]. In the meantime, Michael Kimber, George Milford and John Shilson continued to tend their gardens and livestock.

Many of the hopefuls who rushed to central Otago did make money. Many more did not. Hundreds froze to death in winter snowstorms, which they were poorly equipped to deal with. Death by drowning – in flooded or swift-flowing rivers – became so common that for many years it was referred to as "the Otago disease". Others starved to death when they rushed to the new gold discoveries with little forward preparation. The women who arrived with their husbands were often expected to live in impossible conditions.[51] All that had been predicted by the *Mount Alexander Mail* was found to be true. As reported, the climate *was* abominable. There was not enough gold on any field to retain all who wished to dig.[52] After a fair degree of success and, before the next winter set in, having spent little more than a year at the Otago goldfields, John and Charlotte booked passage on a ship back to Melbourne.

Later in life, John Kimber was interviewed by a reporter to tell of his experiences. The reporter then wrote up the following words:[53]

> "… after a two-year visit to the New Zealand goldfields he returned to Victoria and purchased 130 acres on which he is doing well as a dairy farmer."

---

50 PROV Index of outward passengers to interstate, UK and NZ ports.
51 Cunningham, G 1974, *Guide to the Otago Goldfields Heritage Trail*, pp. 23, 42.
52 Morrell, WP 1968, *The Gold Rushes*, p. 270.
53 Sutherland, A 1888, *Victoria and its Metropolis*, Vol. 2.

While John and Charlotte were in New Zealand during the two years 1863 and 1864, their stay did not extend much beyond twelve months, for John Kimber purchased land in the parish of Faraday on 27th August 1864.[54] This land was just a few hundred yards distance from the holdings of his brother and brothers-in-law, but stretched over the rise into the Long Gully, (now "Quillen Dale") The siblings were living cheek by jowl for the first time since childhood, living and farming in *"the glorious Victorian atmosphere"* on land that so closely resembled their childhood home county. Life at Harcourt was so much better. John Kimber's New Zealand gold finds had the desired effect, for the added riches enabled him to almost double his land holdings from 69 acres to 130 acres, while New Zealand's constant rain and winter cold cured him, forever, of gold fever.

Word from home

In the autumn of 1869, the family at Harcourt received word that their mother Ann Kimber had died on the 7th January. Mrs. Kimber, who was 82 years of age, was buried in the walled churchyard at Bishopsteignton. Charles Kimber informed his siblings that he had ordered a stone monument to be erected over her grave. The monument is located at the right-hand side of the churchyard, in line with the front of the church. It is legible,[55] neatly kept, and has been visited by many of Ann's Australian descendants.

---

54 Land Records and Information Service, Victoria, Title search dossier No. APP 93267G

55 Sighted by the author in 2010 and 2013, by Moira Straw and Meredith Towan, and others.

Tintype photo of Ann Milford

The earliest photo of Ann Milford is a tintype. We may date the photo by the costume; everything points to a date of about 1871. Note that Ann is wearing earrings and a brooch, the ribbon from the bonnet was tied in a spectacular bow adjacent to the collar. The bonnet was a tiny but elaborate confection, perched forward, tilted or on top of the mass of hair. In the fashion of the times the ears were never covered with the hair. The bodice was trimmed

with silk ruches.⁵⁶ This photo was found behind a chimney mantle surround by Terry Hill, "Millbrook" in 2017. Careful not to be seen as a rustic country housewife, Ann is dressed in high fashion. Photographs of Ann taken in the 1890s also show the influence of the latest, elaborate, fashions in women's clothing.

We blush to record

Writing in 1866, James Bonwick, teacher, author, historian and archivist asserts: "... the historian, who is obliged occasionally to fish in dirty water, and who in the pursuit of information is led into strange company, to hear strange things, becomes acquainted with many facts of personal adventure which he blushes to record."

We may have no doubt that the publication of the following advertisement and news articles left the participants feeling ill-used and the subject of a certain amount of unkind comment among their neighbours.

On 14th June 1873 a large advertisement appeared in the *Mount Alexander Mail*.

> **To Mr Martin Penhalurick, Harcourt.**
>
> SIR,—I hereby retract my hasty or unguarded expressions I may have made use of to or respecting you at Harcourt on the 27th ultimo, and assure you that I had no intention of imputing to you any offence whatever, and I now beg to apologise for having used any offensive or annoying expressions on that occasion. You are at perfect liberty to publish this.
> I am, Sir,
> Your obedient servant,
> JOHN KIMBER.
> June 13th, 1873.   633 je 14

---

56 Fletcher, M 1984, *Costume in Australia*, pp. 139, 140, 142.

In order to identify the occasion for this retraction we must turn back the pages of the *Mail* to 4th June 1873 where we find mention of the court proceedings in an assault case brought by Alfred Frost against Martin Penhallurick. Alfred Frost had been at the Talbot Hotel receiving rates for the Shire of Metcalfe in company with Shire Official Collector Mr Douglas. Alfred Frost had long been involved in this task as he was the herdsman and secretary/manager of the Mount Alexander and Faraday Commons with the duty of collecting a per-capita fee for all livestock grazed on public lands in the district.

John Kimber had necessarily taken an interest in this; he had been present at the meetings in 1862 when the Commons were first proclaimed and organised. As a dairyman he was on good terms with the herdsman. On this occasion Alfred Frost was struck by Martin Penhallurick who was alleged to have stated that Alfred Frost had valued his land and that the rates, in consequence of Frost's valuation, were exorbitant. The last straw came when Frost had claimed payment for two dogs, although Penhallurick claimed to own just one. Penhallurick then struck Frost.

Before the matter came to court John Kimber had obviously made some off-hand remarks about the quick-tempered Cornishman.

The verdict of the bench was that Penhallurick had indeed interfered with an officer performing public duties. He was fined 20 shillings plus costs. Smarting at this, Penhallurick then went after John Kimber as a perceived ally of Alfred Frost, and extracted an apology for hasty or unguarded expressions.

When we remember that there were only about forty farmers or householders in Harcourt at the time, we can gauge the intensity of feelings on the matter. Within a few days, talk of the assault case had been replaced by talk of the published apology.

On the following Wednesday a brief paragraph appeared in the

Mail under the heading "Items of News" stating

> "Michael Kimber, dairyman, wishes it known that the public apology in our last Saturday's issue, did not proceed from him, as many persons imagine."

At first sight this is rather un-brotherly behavior, appearing to say "don't point the finger at me", but upon a second reading Michael Kimber might be saying "I would never have apologised to that quick-tempered fellow, no, not in a hundred years."

Six months later, John Kimber brought a case in the Castlemaine Police Court, having summoned John Slaven for Assault. Both parties were represented; Mr. Smyth appeared for John Kimber and Mr. George C Leech for the defendant Slaven.

According to the account of Kimber "… he was driving off his land Slaven's cattle when some angry words concerning them ensued. Suddenly Slaven jumped over the fence and assaulted him."

When George Leech rose to cross examine Kimber he was in a difficult position. John Kimber was known to Leech through the Wesleyan church, Leech being a most able lay preacher and an assiduous visitor of his congregations.

With his inherent respect for the truth, George Leech proceeded through the cross examination and, as reported by the *Mail*:[57]

> "Kimber admitted to having 'peeled to the skin' after the manner of pugilists to make a regular onslaught on his less-than-athletic neighbour. He was only deterred from exhibiting his prowess by an officious neighbour who restrained him from the meditated attack. He

---

57 *Mount Alexander Mail*, 19th December 1873.

also admitted to using opprobrious language towards Slaven. Two witnesses saw Slaven jump over the fence and strike Kimber but neither knew of anything that passed antecedent to provoke the quarrel. Mr. Leech explained that, if he wished to encourage litigation, he would have advised his client to take out a cross-summons for assault. He called upon the daughter of Slaven to take the witness stand –she stated that Kimber had set the dogs on her father's cattle and that his land was unfenced. It was difficult to stay the cattle from going on it; and that he had used foul language towards her father."

At this stage the bench realised that there were faults on both sides and dismissed the case. No costs were allowed on either side. Where was Kimber's legal counsel in all of this? In his own way George Leech had taken over the entire case, his only desire being to bring peace between two neighbours and achieve the most Christian outcome. In all likelihood, John Slaven had lost all self-control when his animals and his daughter were subjected to strong language by John Kimber. Probably both men felt foolish over the incident and knew that there was much behind-hand talk about them in the district. People have sold their homes and left the district after such a happening, or have retired from the public eye after an excess of temper such as had been displayed on this occasion. But Leech wanted to retain John Kimber as a member of his congregation and so defended Slaven only to the extent of pointing out the parity of the situation. Neither man won and neither lost. Blessed indeed are the peacemakers.

To me, the most enduring aspect of this little scene is the word picture of John Kimber, 48 years of age, peeled to the skin and, compared to his neighbor, with the figure of an athlete.

Of course we call to mind the saying that "good fences make good neighbours" and we must remember that fencing wire was not then generally available. Given that there were only two near neighbours, only one of whom was related, it is probable that the man who held John Kimber back from committing his intended assault was George Milford.

... that with dauntless breast the little tyrant of his fields withstood[58]

We come close to George Milford the man of principle in the next chapter of his life story. He stood in the long line of descent from those who, at Runnymede on 15th June 1215, forced their King to seal the Great Charter. George's stand against authority is consistent with the actions of the great English parliamentarian John Hampden, whose refusal to pay the Ship Tax was one of the sparks that set alight the Civil War in which King Charles lost his throne and his life. Another catalyst for war was Charles' ill-considered and abortive attempt to arrest the five outstanding leaders of the Commons. Two of the five were Devon men.[59]

These two incidents reveal the response of a Devon man to official bullying and highlight the need for every generation to stand up for its rights.

From 1877 there was agitation in the Barkers Creek community to petition for a supply of water with which to sluice for gold. It was claimed that there was plenty of gold-bearing ground at Barkers Creek, enough to employ hundreds of miners if they had a constant

---

58 From *Elegy, written in a country churchyard* by Thomas Gray.

59 Sellman, RR 1985, *Aspects of Devon History*, Devon Books, Exeter, p. 36.

supply of water. Eventually it was considered feasible to bring water from Porter's Tunnel at Faraday to the head of Specimen Gully. In October 1880, the Minister for Mines visited Specimen Gully to see for himself the proposed route of the channel. After this visit the Minister agreed to put the cost of a channel in the Government estimates.

In the winter of 1881, a trench along the contours – two feet wide and two feet deep – was dug by the miners "with alacrity never hitherto obtained in this district". The race passed through much privately-owned land, meandering around the hillsides and emerging at the head of Specimen Gully. In the meantime, thirty miners had set up their timber sluice boxes and eagerly awaited the water. The water had been turned on at Faraday in the first week of October 1881 but, after two weeks, no water had arrived in Specimen Gully. At last someone walked back along the race to meet the water. They did not have far to walk to find the cause of the stoppage. Where the channel rounded the slate ridge, to their surprise, they found the race had been filled in, by some person, or persons, unknown.

In calculating the expense of providing water to the sluicers of Barkers Creek, the Office of Mines had left one vital expense out of the estimate. They did not intend to pay compensation to landholders for the land needed to give an easement for the water channel. The wording of land titles reserved to the Crown the right to use the land for purposes incidental to gold mining. It was the opinion of the Office of Mines that property owners should be prepared to sacrifice their land in the public interest. The Office also stated, had they known that landholders would be seeking exorbitant compensation for their land, the Office would have reconsidered the case for construction. This was a classic case of official bullying.

Harcourt and Faraday landowners *did* seek compensation. One had gone to the length of filling in the newly constructed water race where it crossed his land. The *Mail* was quick to point out that thirty miners were waiting for the arrival of the water. In response, a letter appeared in the *Mail* on 25th October 1881 to explain the land-owner's position.

> "Sir, Having seen a paragraph in your paper stating that I would not let water pass through my land at Harcourt, and thirty men were thrown idle because I would not accept fair compensation, allow me to inform you that I was never offered one shilling, and I can assure you it is no fault of mine the water has not been running these two months. You should saddle the right man with the blame. —Yours, &c,
>
> G Milford,
>
> Harcourt, October, 24th, 1881." [60]

A valuator from Melbourne resolved the matter and the sluices started operating in November. The lower reaches of Specimen Gully still, more than a century and a quarter later, show the effects of their operations.

The Office of Mines did not learn from this. Two years later there was a proposal to extend the channel, from the Specimen Gully race into the Harcourt valley along the foot of Mount Alexander. The Office wrote to the Metcalfe Shire pointing out that certain of the property holders, through whose land it is proposed to construct the race, have notified their intention to claim compensation, thus

---

[60] I told this story during the emotionally draining period when VicRoads was planning to resume thirty-eight properties in Harcourt to build the Calder Freeway. The moral was not lost on the audience, who enthusiastically said "Good on him!"

hindering the Office's work. The property owners should have surrendered their land with no recompense, for the greater public good. The Office called on the Shire to facilitate the creation of an easement, otherwise the Office would re-consider the matter. Councillors James Lang and George Symes, who did not approve of the high-handed spirit of the Office's letter, were deputised to discuss the situation with the landholders.[61]

Councillors Symes and Lang then made a beeline (so to speak) for George Milford and John Kimber to get the full story. The two men pointed out that they would definitely need compensation; the line of the race would wind about in a zigzag manner when crossing their gardens (orchards), and would divide their land somewhat. Other landowners along the route were interviewed. Mr. Cundy, Mr. Blair and Mr. Parbett were all asking £5 per acre, which was considered reasonable.[62]

> cost for land required, and yesterday they visited first Mr John Kimber, and found the race passed through his garden and cultivated land in a zig-zag course, about 15 chains in length, cutting up his property a good deal, for which he only asks L10. They proceeded to Mr Milford's, and there found the line of race to wind about in crossing through his cultivated paddock of 33½ acres, completely destroying the property for cultivation. It was thought that about two acres of land would be required from Mr Milford, for which he asked L25, which, considering the cutting in two of the paddocks, was very reasonable. Mr Cundy was next visited,

In due course, the easements were created, compensation paid and the Harcourt Gardens Race started to deliver irrigation water. This was a great boon to the orchardists, providing water from the Malmsbury Reservoir to sustain the fruit trees throughout the

---

61 *Mount Alexander Mail,* 4th October 1883.
62 *Mount Alexander Mail,* 27th October 1883.

summer. Gravity furrow irrigation was a big advance on the old method of carting water to each tree. Having accepted compensation for the easement, Messrs Lang, Kimber and Milford were among the first to sign-up to take a regular allocation of water! Using a single furrow plough, the orchardist created a downhill furrow past the base of each tree, incidentally providing a summer pastime for their children and grandchildren who delighted in sending small bark boats sailing down the furrows.

Family matters: the boys provided for

The Shilsons lived above the water race at the very head of Specimen Gully. They were adherents of the Bible Christian Church in Specimen Gully, which amalgamated with the Wesleyans of Barkers Creek in 1871, where John taught in the Sabbath School. In the bible that he had brought from "Home", the treasury of Christ's

Jane Shilson.

sayings, "The Sermon on the Mount" is marked and underlined. In 1876 the Bible Christians of Faraday had purchased and erected a brick church, formerly situated at Elphinstone. John Kimber was a Trustee of this latter church and it is probable that John and Jane Shilson attended Faraday church thereafter.

From about 1880, Jane Shilson made repeated requests to her sister Ann Milford, asking for her nephew William Milford to live at "Mount View" with his aunt and uncle. Jane and John had taken a liking to young Bill, then aged about 13, and, as they were childless, they intended to adopt him. For some years Ann and George resisted this request; they wished their son to grow up with his brothers and sister. However, after Bill had finished at Harcourt Primary School, he was sent to work with his uncle during seasonal peak times, staying overnight at their home on the hill.

Soon it was understood that he would live permanently at "Mount View", eventually to inherit the Shilson's land and orchard.

In going to "Mount View", Bill was going to a remote farmlet with primitive amenities. Cooking arrangements at Mount View remained unchanged for the duration of the home's existence. All the cooking was done over an open fire – pots were hung above the flames on chains of varying lengths built right into the chimney, or they were hooked onto a hinged pot-hanger that swung out from the side of the fireplace.[63]

For Ann and George Milford, brought up to work on a large farm away from home from an early age, it most likely seemed not far from their own experience to let their son move into another household. But it was a step taken with reluctance, a step viewed by the next generation as unusual.

Letters from Devon brought unwelcome news in 1883 that George's sister, Sophia Vicary, had died. But George was forward looking both

---
63 Sighted in the house ruins by David and George Milford, April 1967.

in his daily work and his planning for the next generation.

Ann and George's eldest son, Thomas, obtained employment with Duncan Ferries, stonemason, who had opened a yard in Harcourt in 1880. Tom learned every aspect of the trade and was soon engaged under indentures. Steam polishing and sawing of stone for monuments was one aspect of the trade. Erecting and lettering cemetery monuments took him to many districts as the Ferries business came to be a leading supplier in central Victoria. Distinctive Harcourt granite monuments with the Ferries label are to be found in all regional cemeteries.[64] Tom was a good cricketer, particularly handy with the bat. His name appears in many reports of cricket matches.

Cricket was a serious pastime, the game fostering many good qualities. A cricketer cultivated a keen eye, a steady hand, a stout heart, strong limbs, with activity, coolness and precision.[65] The young men of Harcourt, toiling during the week at their family orchards, valued the sport for its social and community-building values.

While Tom was learning the stonemason's trade, John Milford was engaged with his father in laying out an orchard on the lower slopes of a twenty-acre allotment on Faraday Road opposite to the homestead. This was done with the stated intention that this would be John's property when his father retired from active work. The land was known as "John Milford's garden". One of the first trees planted by John was a Mulberry. It is still to be seen in the 21st century.

A precious relic of this time is a beautifully bound volume of Sacred Biography and History illustrated with steel engravings,

---

64 The foundation date carved in granite on the porch of Harcourt Methodist Church is Tom's handiwork. This work was done in 1934.

65 Brodie, JC, *The Victorian Cricketers Guide for 1860-61*.

which belonged to George Milford and provided much Sunday reading. All the first generation of Milford children attended the Wesleyan Sunday School in Harcourt when young. Their Kimber cousins were brought up as Anglicans, despite their mother having

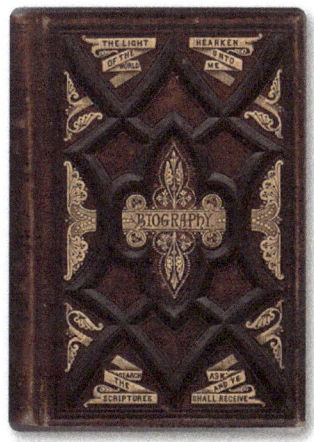

Sacred Biography and History.

Tom and Eliza with their children.

been a Roman Catholic. Sectarianism was never a big issue in the family. Tom Milford became an adherent of the Plymouth Brethren in the years when Henry Robert Bastow was locally influential (1892-1920). Eliza Milford, Elizabeth and John Milford, with their families, were active members of the Harcourt Methodist Church. Amos Milford's children were all to be brought up to attend Harcourt Church of Christ where they mixed with their extended Symes family relations.

A prune-coloured silk wedding dress

> **MARRIED.**
> FROST—MILFORD.—On the 26th inst., at the Wesleyan Church, Harcourt, by the Rev. J. Lowe, George, second son of the late Alfred Frost, Esq., of Durham Ox, to Jane Kimber Milford, only daughter of George Milford, Esq., of Harcourt.

In August 1885,[66] the *Mount Alexander Mail* reported that

> "... a marriage ceremony that created a great deal of interest was performed at the Wesleyan Church, Harcourt on Wednesday last, by the Rev. J. Lowe, when Miss J. K. Milford, of Harcourt, was united to Mr. George Frost, of Durham Ox. The bride, who had been a teacher and sewing mistress at the State School, Faraday for some time past, looked handsome in a prune coloured silk dress, with point lace, veil and the orthodox orange blossom. There

---

66 *Mount Alexander Mail*, 31st August 1885.

were four bridesmaids, who were also prettily attired. The church was crowded to excess, and as the bridal party were leaving the building, Miss Healy played Mendehllsohn's 'Wedding March' on the organ. The couple left in the evening for Melbourne."

Alfred Frost, with his wife Anne and family of seven, had left Harcourt in 1877 to settle at Canary Island, on the Loddon River near Durham Ox. Canary Island, formed by the Loddon River and the Twelve Mile Creek, is about half a mile wide and six miles long. George and Jane Frost made their home at Canary Island on a 320 acre block. When it became fashionable to give a name to a home,[67] Jane and George named their Canary Island residence "Kimberville". From 1893 to 1900 George Frost and Charles

Jinnie Frost.

---

67 This must have been in the first decade of the 1900s. Eliza and Tom named their home "Millbrook", John and Elizabeth's was named "Brooklyn" while Nell and Amos named theirs "Craig Elvan". When I was a child, birthday cards and Christmas cards would come from "all at Craig Elvan".

Milford held the lease of a 440 acre dairy farm at Canary Island. This was a sizeable operation with sixty dairy cows, two bulls, upwards of thirty pigs, cream cans, steam separator and boiler, etc. The dairy farm, known as "Baker's", must have required continuous work and would have caused much worry in dry years. The whole Frost and Milford Dairy undertaking was sold by auction upon the expiry of the seven-year lease.[68]

Tom and Eliza's house.

Jane's brother, Charles Milford, purchased a similarly sized block adjacent to his sister's land and lived with the Frosts, growing wheat and raising fat cattle for sale in Bendigo while still retaining an interest in the family home at Harcourt. After 1900, Charlie regularly assisted his brothers Bill, John and Amos in their orchards and, in partnership with Amos, worked an eight-acre orchard on the east side of the Faraday Road. In practice, this meant that Charlie

---

68 Auction Sale display advertisement dated 9th May 1900.

lived with Amos from February to June and lived the other half of the year with Jane and George Frost.

In the 1890s, Tom and Amos regularly travelled to Canary Island to stay for long periods. It is said that this was because their mother was in poor health. The journey, in a buggy, took an afternoon and all the next day, with an overnight stop in Bendigo.[69] It is recorded that T, C and A Milford played cricket for Yando at this time.[70] No doubt they also helped with the daily milking.

Besides farming, George Frost was a bridge builder and constructed many bridges over the many creeks for the local shire

Charlie Milford.

69 Information by Les Milford.
70 Stevens, FH 1969, *Smoke from the Hill: a history of the Boort District 1836–1968*, Boort Historical Society, Bendigo.

council. A newspaper article reporting on a new bridge over the Loddon River built by Mr. G Frost states that this bridge reflects great credit on both engineer and contractor. [71]

When they retired, George and Jane Frost and Charles Milford sold the land at Canary Island. A report of their farewell from Canary Island appeared in the local paper, the *Pyramid Hill Advertiser*, dated April 24, 1914. They bought land at Shelbourne East, which they farmed while living at Camp Street, Kangaroo Flat.[72]

New Year's Day 1889

The *Mount Alexander Mail* reported:

> "The New Year's Day in Castlemaine, which opened with rejoicing, closed calamitously by the loss of several lives, occasioned by the most disastrous flood that has occurred in the district for many years. A little after three o'clock the rain poured down in almost a deluge and continued without intermission till about half-past five o'clock."

It was not until nine days later that the newspaper reported the actual amount of rainfall – five and three-quarter inches of rain had fallen with such intensity that it ran off immediately, causing flooding in every little creek and gully. Forest Creek and Barkers Creek rose quickly. Evidence of the force and volume of water was seen everywhere. Serious damage was done to the structure of, or the approaches to, every bridge in the West Riding of Metcalfe

---
71   *Pyramid Hill Advertiser,* August 9th 1895.
72   Now 4 Olympic Parade, Kangaroo Flat.

> Harcourt
> 29th January 1889
>
> The President and Councillors
> of the United Shire of Metcalfe,
>
> Sir and Gentlemen,
> I beg to inform you through not having a culvert fenced on a Public road in the West Riding of Metcalfe returning to my home on 1st January 1889 I met with a bad accident my horse drowned buggy smashed, myself, wife, and son, had a narrow escape from being drowned I am sure the accident would not have happened if the culvert had rails on —
> I hope you will favourably receive my letter and allow me (£20) twenty pounds for my loss
>
> I am
> Gentlemen
> Yours respectfully
> Geo Milford

Shire, while every bridge in Castlemaine township was carried away by the impact of floating trees and debris.

Ann and George Milford, with their youngest son Amos, had been visiting friends in Castlemaine. As they were returning home along Black Jack Road, just beyond Lupton's Live and Let Live Hotel, they saw water flowing across the road. George whipped the horse to drive through, but the horse lost its footing and tumbled into the raging torrent. The horse drowned, the buggy was smashed and the three occupants scrambled out of danger. Ann, handicapped by her long skirt, had a narrow escape from drowning. The bedraggled trio walked back to the Live and Let Live Hotel to dry out and to wait until the rain stopped and the water subsided before walking home.

The appended letter to the Shire of Metcalfe[73] sought recompense as, in George's opinion, the accident would not have happened if the culvert had had handrails. There is no record of the Shire agreeing to this request.

John Kimber moves to Castlemaine

> Mr Kimber, who sold his orchard at Harcourt to Mr Symes, proposes taking a little leisure after his many years of close industry, and has for the purpose of enjoying his retirement purchased a house in Doveton-street from Mr H. Lane, where he will henceforth reside.

In March 1892, John and Charlotte Kimber sold their orchard to Mr. William Symes with the intention of taking a little leisure after their many years of hard work. John Kimber purchased a brick house at 49-51 Doveton Street from Mr. Henry Lane in which to live in his retirement.[74] There was an extra allotment in the purchase, which John Kimber used for his horse and garden. Having sold his property at Faraday, John Kimber organised a clearing sale. Once again we can see the extent of his farming; the sale included Spring

73 Castlemaine Historical Society Inc archives, Met18 Bag 23.
74 *Mount Alexander Mail*, 18th March 1892.

Cart, Dray, Harness, Ploughs, Chaff-cutter, Weighbridge, Horses, Cows, Pigs, Poultry and a lot of sundries.[75]

> **Lascelles & Adams' Advts.**
>
> LASCELLES & ADAMS have been favoured with instructions from MR KIMBER, of Harcourt,
>
> TO SELL BY PUBLIC AUCTION
>
> On
>
> **Wednesday, March 23rd,**
>
> On the Premises,
> At 2 o'clock,
>
> A Clearing Sale of Stock Implements, Spring Cart, Dray, Harness, Ploughs, Harrows, Chaff-cutter, Weighbridge, Horses, Cows, Pigs, Poultry, and a lot of sundries, in consequence of having sold his property. The whole will be for
> ABSOLUTE SALE WITHOUT RESERVE.
>
> mh 16 19 22 23

John Henry Kimber

Ann and George's next door neighbor, Michael Kimber, was one of those who supplied wood to the Victorian Railways. The wood, in five-foot lengths, was to be delivered to the Barkers Creek rail siding. One day, while felling a gum tree in the bush, Michael's eldest son John Henry was struck by a falling branch. He was then aged 24 and had been out of sorts and losing weight for some time. The blow from the tree seemed to precipitate a crisis. Medical help was sought when he developed swelling and an abscess on his back. The doctor diagnosed "caries of the spine" and arranged that the young man be admitted to Castlemaine Hospital on 5th September 1893. John Henry was discharged from Hospital on 22nd December 1893, with his medical record being marked "relieved".[76]

75 *Mount Alexander Mail,* 16th March 1892.
76 Castlemaine Hospital Record held by CHSI.

It is touching to think that John Henry was taken home for Christmas. The fact that his illness was a form of Tuberculosis[77] was probably not realised. The torment of a ride from Castlemaine to Harcourt in a spring cart can only be imagined. John Henry's wasted frame would have been a source of worry to his sisters and brothers. His siblings were aged from 29 to 13 at this time.

The destructive disease persisted in its course. John Henry was again admitted to Hospital on 2nd January 1894, ten days after his discharge. The custom of those days was for relatives to live at the hospital to tend the patient. This was unavailing. John Henry suffered the collapse of a vertebra and so much spinal damage that he became a paraplegic at age 25.[78] He died on 7th February, just five weeks after re-admission to Hospital.

> **Funeral Notice.**
>
> THE Friends of Mr M. Kimber are respectfully invited to follow the remains of his late beloved son, John Henry, aged 25 years, to the place of interment, the Harcourt Cemetery.
> The cortege will move from his residence, Harcourt, TO-MORROW (Friday), at 2.30 p.m.
> NIEBUHR & SON,
> Undertakers.

John Henry was the eldest son, named in memory of a loved but childless uncle. John Henry's death, blamed on the tree,[79] was keenly felt. Though no artist was present to depict his burial at the Harcourt cemetery, we can paint the scene in our imagination, as the acid-etched, gold-leafed, horsedrawn hearse made its way

---

77 It is now known as Potts Disease (Spine).
78 We are indebted to Dr Charles Kerr for the diagnosis (2014) and advice re the progress of the disease.
79 Information from Leslie Milford.

across the grassy graveyard to the lonely north-west corner of the cemetery. His tearful parents, aunts, uncles, siblings, brothers-in-law and cousins were on hand, giving support, stonily watching.[80]

John Henry's grave was the first of his family's burials here, this was the first death of an adult in the extended family after more than thirty-five years in Victoria. An assemblage of sixty buggies and carriages at the funeral indicates a crowd in excess of two hundred mourners. Tethering sixty and more horses must have been a complex exercise in itself.

The burial service was conducted by the Rev Archdeacon Crawford of the Church of England on that fine summer afternoon.

> The funeral of the young man John Henry Kimber took place yesterday and was numerously attended, there being upwards of 60 vehicles in the cortege, thus testifying to the great esteem in which the deceased was held. At the grave, in the Harcourt cemetery, the burial service was read by the Rev E. A. Crawford. The funeral arrangements were satisfactorily carried out by Messrs Niebuhr and Son. The deceased succumbed to disease of the spine, and for six months was a patient in the Hospital.

Money worries in the 1890s

The Milford family banked with the leading government-backed Savings Banks at Castlemaine. During the early 1890s these banks experienced difficult times and were in great danger of ceasing operations entirely.

The Victorian Post Office Savings Bank closed its doors and suspended payments in the early 1890s. The bank had acted as an independent enterprise with very little control or supervision. The little people put in and the big people took out. Too often the funds

---

80 *Mount Alexander Mail*, 8th February 1894 and later issues.

were foolishly lent, sometimes on little security, to speculators with a glib story. The PO Savings Bank was not alone in this. The regime of the Savings Bank Commissioners was to prove extremely damaging to the interests of depositors. It was a time of universal speculation. Every Victorian town and city has examples of ostentatious buildings erected in this "boom period". The Commissioners lent money to fund the construction of magnificent buildings in Melbourne, loans which would take years to be repaid. As far as the Post Office Savings Bank was concerned, it had handed all of its depositors' money to successive State Treasurers who blithely used most of it on current government expenditure.

Beset by a multitude of troubles, the Patterson Government had taken no action. When the Turner Government swept the polls in 1894, one of its first actions was to attempt to clean up the chaos in the two savings banks. After legislation (which took years to pass both houses) the Commissioners Savings Banks and the the Post Office Savings Bank were amalgamated to form the State Savings Bank of Victoria.[81]

The Milford passbooks, which commence in 1898, show when this amalgamation took effect. Passbooks of George Milford and Amos Milford in my possession commence in the year 1898 with the entry "Transferred from POS bank", the amounts being £20/3/1 and £32/2/2 respectively.

Getting much of their food and fuel through their own effort, the Harcourt farmers might go for weeks without needing any significant sum. They certainly did not have much use for banks. A little money put by was a convenience. When it was wanted it was wanted in lump sums; ten shillings now, say, for a little pig, then fifteen shillings or so in six weeks' time to shoe a horse or mend

---

[81] Cannon, M 1967, *The Land Boomers*, Melbourne University Press, pp. 198–200.

a cart, and so on. The bank books of George and Ann each show four or five cheques paid in to the passbooks in the period July to October each year. This would represent bulk sales of fruit or end-of-season settlements. No other records survive to indicate the name or location of the buyer or fruit merchant, but these cheques are probably the proceeds of fruit sold to Bendigo greengrocers, sold in large quantities into the Melbourne market or consigned to England.[82] Local sales would have been of individual boxes of fruit sold for cash. It is certain that cash was hidden away at home because the banks were proven to be untrustworthy.

Income was seasonal and only came in when the fruit was saleable – from March to September. For the home, vegetables and fruit were readily available, the cow provided milk, cream and butter, the pig provided the flitches of bacon, and wine was homemade. The hay grown in the paddock could be stockpiled for horsefeed, firewood was free for the taking, and soap could be made from the wood-ash. The purse was not subject to the same constant drain as that of the modern householder.[83] It was for these reasons that the Milford

Milford pigs.

---

82 Neighbour James Lang, with his father-in-law Henry Ely, had pioneered the export of Harcourt apples in the late 1880s.

83 This paragraph owes a lot to Bourne, G 1912, *Change in the Village*, pp. 80, 81.

family and their Harcourt neighbours passed through the depression of the 1890s relatively unscathed, while, in the cities, unemployment, homelessness, poverty, starvation, disease and family break-up were terrifyingly common.

Photographs

Mrs Sarah Ann Milford.

Among the family archives is a notable photo dating from about 1896. It depicts Mrs Sarah Ann Milford, then aged 65, in a buggy somewhere in Castlemaine. The horse is equipped with light buggy harness and wearing a buggy bridle. Mrs Milford is holding the reins in gloved hands, having driven five miles into town from her home on the Faraday Road, Harcourt. The journey would have taken about an hour. Mrs Milford is wearing a strictly tailored "must fit snug everywhere" jacket with shoulder cape, very full sleeves, closely buttoned bodice, high neckline and rather severe collar.

This was high fashion. The separate skirt was of lined, brown twill cotton, with a pocket at the side toward the back. A buggy rug is strapped across her legs. The buggy rug, waterproof on the outside, had a black cloth lining, heavily embroidered in a yellow stylised floral pattern. I know it is yellow – I remember being wrapped in it when I was very young.

Despite the masculine-oriented property laws and society norms, many Victorian women were active partners in their family business. The photo is a good record of the fashions, transport and capabilities of this pioneer.

Another photograph from this time depicts Tom Milford and his wife, Eliza Laura Loveland, of Bendigo. Tom and Eliza were married at Forest Street Wesleyan Church, Bendigo, on 6th January

Tom and Eliza Milford.

1897. The Forest Street church is on a steeply sloping hillside. Tom and Eliza made their home on steeply sloping land at Harcourt, building on a triangular block given to them by George Milford. The front of their home is six feet above ground at the north-east corner. Tom worked the orchard on this hillside while carrying on his work as a stonemason.

Up on the mountain

Mount Alexander was close by. For many years the granite mountain was a source of timber and a farmers' common. Harcourt people roamed freely over the western slope and along the ridge. For a small fee they could graze their cattle on the mountain. The cattle created well worn paths on the easier slopes. There was no permanent water on the mountain, and this restricted the range over which the cattle could graze. Church and ANA Picnics were held in Picnic Gully at the foot of the mount, directly to the east of the State School. A favourite Sunday afternoon walk in the cooler months was to Dog Rocks at the southern end of the mount or, a somewhat longer walk, to the summit, where a granite Cairn had been erected in 1876 to mark the starting point for a trigonometric survey.

Local residents casually refer to this cairn as a Boer War memorial. People with a precise interest in history will note that the cairn was built over twenty years before the Boer War. However, there is value in the oral history as it fixes this as the site for the district celebrations for the relief of Mafeking and the end of the South African war. Mafeking was a small town in up-country Bechuanaland. It was besieged by local forces on 12th October 1899 as the opening act of war. The Boer Free State Army then attacked the British and inflicted a series of disastrous defeats on Britain's leading army generals and their troops. After the depressing spectacle of large British forces failing to make headway against smaller numbers of Boers, it was a relief to the British press to find that a small British garrison was holding out against a larger number of Boers. Gallant little Mafeking and its commander, Colonel Robert Baden-Powell, remote from all help, were just what the nation needed. Was the garrison doomed? Would Colonel Baden-Powell become another British martyr? After seven months of starvation and daily bombardment, Mafeking was relieved by an advance party of British troops on 17th May 1900.

In Castlemaine, Victoria, the editor of the *Mail* wrote: "Inspired by a right spirit the young men of the district have arranged next Friday to prepare a huge bonfire on the summit of Mount Alexander, to be lit when news arrives that the British have taken Pretoria or peace is declared."

Amos Milford was among the twenty young men "of right spirit" who spent a total of four days building the pile of branches, reckoned to be the biggest bonfire in the colony. There were no roads on the mountain in those days, so the climb to the summit would have meant a one hour walk. The reader, who is more than 100 years distant from the event, might consider it to be "environmental vandalism" to expend eighty man-days in gathering up fallen branches to be burnt. It shows the depth of community angst over the loss of British prestige that men were prepared to do this.

On June 5th 1900, British troops occupied Pretoria. Field Marshall Lord Roberts had occupied Johannesburg, and the gold mines were securely in the possession of the British. On June 6th, the bonfire on the top of Mount Alexander was set alight, in the presence of a large number of locals, and was visible for a very great distance. The spectators joined in heartily, singing "God Save the Queen" and "Rule Britannia".

The land beyond goodbye[84]

After the death of John Shilson in 1896, his wife Jane saw to it that a granite memorial was erected over his grave. This memorial is inscribed with four lines of what we might describe as a moralising verse. Harcourt Cemetery has many substantial memorials, but such verses are rarely to be found among them. Perhaps Jane was thinking back to the loss of John Henry Kimber when she gave these lines to the stonemason:

> We cannot tell who next may fall
> Beneath thy chastening rod.
> One must be first but we must all
> Prepare to meet our God.

Jane Shilson died, aged 79, at Faraday, of septic absorption following gangrene of the leg, on 9th September 1898. Ann Milford died, at Harcourt, aged 69, of nephritis (kidney disease) on 18th September 1900, Michael Kimber died, aged 74, at Harcourt, of heart failure and dropsy, 12th April 1901 and John Kimber died, age 75, at his home in Doveton Street, Castlemaine on 10th October 1902. (John Shilson and Charlotte Kimber had predeceased their spouses.) In the space of six years, all of the Devon folk, except George Milford, had died.

After Ann died, George decided to retire from active work, and his sons George Amos and Charles worked his lands and retained all the profits. In return, the two sons looked after their father, who resided with them, but they paid no fixed rent for the use of the

---

84 "The Land Beyond Goodbye" is a verse, full of pathos, by Will H Ogilvie in the volume *Hearts of Gold and Other Verses* (1912). Another Victorian euphemism for death was "joined the great majority", a phrase much used by the *Mount Alexander Mail*.

land.[85] George, who suffered from rheumatism,[86] lived for thirteen years after Ann's passing.

In the orchard

Bill Milford managed the orchard which had been established by John and Jane Shilson. This was an orchard typical of a small-holding in Harcourt. It had a wide range of fruit trees; pears, apples, plums, cherries, figs, apricots, peaches and almonds.

Down in the valley, the other Milford orchards tended to be more restricted in the types of fruit grown, growing more apples and pears. Their objective was to grow uniform-sized, fancy-grade (unblemished) fruit. This was far more profitable than cultivating a multitude of varieties. The principal varieties grown in the oldest part of the orchard were;-

- Rymer; an early maturing round, slightly flattened apple that has dull red stripes and blush and a dark-green skin base colour. The yellow flesh is crisp and juicy and well-flavoured. It keeps well and can be used for eating or cooking. The oldest trees in the orchard were Rymers; they had a straight trunk, branching out about three feet above the ground, and were vigorous and productive.
- Sturmer Pippin; Conical in shape, greenish yellow. The taste is very tart unless left to fully mature on the tree. Mainly used for cooking. A constant bearer and a long keeper.
- Cleopatra;[87] a golden-yellow, mid-season apple with white flesh, tasty, crisp and crunchy.

---

85 Probate Inventory, George Milford VPRS 28/P3 Unit 368 Item 129/521.
86 *Mount Alexander Mail,* 1st October 1894.
87 *Mount Alexander Mail,* 9th June 1906.

- Munroe's Favourite;[88] a late apple, flattened in shape, with a greenish skin, excellent for cooking and with exceptional keeping qualities.
- Esopus Spitzenberg;[89] an American variety with an excellent flavour which improves with storage. Similar to today's Jazz.

There were many other varieties found in a small orchard. The Milford orchards were characterised by the commercial need to produce a large quantity of each single variety and thus these particular orchards had fewer varieties.

A and C Milford exported their fruit to England and Germany. They were encouraged to do this from 1906 onwards by James R Warren, newly appointed agent for Lohmann and Co, Melbourne. J R Warren had previously lived in Harcourt. It was reported in the press that:

> "… A and C Milford have studied the wants of this market best; it is the best sort [of fruit] which pay the grower and inferior stuff ought not to be shipped to this market. As the ship freight, lighterage, wharfage dues, receiving, delivery, warehousing and commission will average less than 5s [five shillings] per case, the results cannot be other than satisfactory to those growers"[90]

A photo from this era depicts Milford lorries at the Harcourt Railway station, where their fruit is being despatched to the port while the horses stand patiently in the shafts.

---

88 *Mount Alexander Mail*, 9th June 1906.
89 *Mount Alexander Mail*, 27th May 1910.
90 *Mount Alexander Mail*, 9th June 1906.

Milford fruit at the railways.

Waiting to load up.

A dangerous business

The utter dependence of society on the horse occasionally involved some spectacular and dangerous "bolts". There are two examples from our family story.

In September 1901, John Milford had taken a cart laden with hay to the market square in Castlemaine. He got off to attend to some business and then returned to his cart with the intention of taking the hay to its destination. He had barely got onto his cart when the horse sped away, and when crossing a gutter in the Market Square, jolted John from the cart with great force. He was taken to Woolnough's blacksmith's shop in a very dazed condition. As he appeared to be getting worse, Mr. Woolnough took him to his own home where John became insensible and remained unconscious for three hours. He was then taken to his home at Harcourt.[91]

A few years later Charles Milford was travelling to his land at Canary Island. He had started on the journey with a spring cart and a pair of horses. When about four miles from Durham Ox the horse on the outrigger rubbed his winkers off on the shafts of the cart and, starting the other horse with it, they bolted for a distance of eight miles (twelve kilometres on straight roads across flat country) when the cart was overturned. Little damage was done, Charlie being mercifully landed in a very muddy place.[92]

One wonders whether words passed between the brothers after these incidents. Amos Milford had a reputation for breaking-in young horses.

My father said that Amos had very skillful roping techniques. The fact that Amos never hit the headlines, in an age when a spectacular bolt was headline news, must reinforce our estimation of him as a competent horse-tamer.

> **District Correspondence.**
>
> **HARCOURT.**
>
> Mr C. Milford had rather a sensational experience last week. Owning land at Canary Island he is obliged to periodically visit it. He had started on one of these visits with a spring cart and pair of horses. When about four miles from Durham Ox the horse on the outrigger rubbed the winkers off on the shafts of the cart, and starting the other horse with it they bolted for a distance of eight miles, when the cart was overturned. Little damage was done, Mr Milford being mercifully landed in a very muddy place.

---

91 *Mount Alexander Mail,* 5th September 1901.
92 *Mount Alexander Mail,* 18th July 1907.

> A slight sensation was caused in Market Square yesterday afternoon. Three carts laden with chaff were standing in the Square, and the drivers, who had been attending to business in the town, returned with the intention of taking the chaff to its destination. The first driver had hardly got on to his cart when the horses bolted, but luckily were checked by the fence from going very far. The second driver had just got up, when off his team went, but he managed to pull the horses up. The third driver, Mr John Milford, of Harcourt, had barely got on to his cart when the horses went away, and when crossing a gutter in the Square jolted Mr Milford from the cart on to the ground with great force. He was put in a cab by Constable Walsh with the intention of being taken to a doctor, but at his own request he was taken to Mr W. Woolnough's blacksmith's shop in a very dazed condition. As he appeared to get worse he was taken to Mr Woolnough's private house, where he became insensible, and remained in that state for three hours. On regaining consciousness he was removed to his home at Harcourt.

Another feature of the era of the horse was the need to harness the animal before undertaking a task like ploughing, spraying or moving fruit or before setting out on a journey in the spring cart or the buggy. A horse in regular use in the shafts was kept on chaff in the stable[93] so as to be quickly fitted out with bridle and harness. Draught horses were kept in small paddocks. Fenced paddocks were reserved for working horses, while cattle (each fitted with a cowbell) were routinely turned out on the roads and onto the farmers' commons after milking each morning. It was a regular chore for the children to bring home the cattle after school each day.

---

93 The stable was a timber building with half-doors abutting the apple house.

Amos and Edith

Exactly six months after Ann Milford's death, a very pretty wedding was celebrated at Faraday. This was in the last week of March 1901, the contracting parties being Mr. Amos Milford, son of Mr. George Milford, an old resident of this district, and Miss Edith Symes, daughter of Mr. James Symes, the well-known fruit grower of Harcourt. The couple were united by the Rev A. Powell, of Castlemaine. In the evening the happy pair departed for Ballarat

Amos and Edith Milford.

> **FARADAY.**
> A very pretty wedding was celebrated here during the past week, the contracting parties being Mr Amos Milford, son of Mr George Milford, an old resident of this district, and Miss Edith Symes, daughter of Mr James Symes, the well-known fruitgrower of Harcourt. The couple were united by the Rev A. Powell, of Castlemaine. In the evening the happy pair departed for Ballarat where they intend spending their honeymoon.

where they intend spending their honeymoon.[94] A son, named George Stanley Milford, was born on 22nd April 1902.

Photographs of Edith and of her sister-in-law and neighbour Eliza depict them as lively, well-dressed women who must have made for happy homes and a busy social life for the Milford menfolk.

On Friday 7th April 1905, Edith Milford, 24 years of age, went to a neighbour's house in Black Jack Road to get some honey. Her path took her walking through an orchard in which there were beehives. When Amos came home for dinner, he found his wife absent and three-year-old Stanley, who was being looked after by his grandfather, crying for his mother.

Amos went in search of Edith and 200 yards from the house he discovered his wife lying face downwards on the ground, moaning, in an unconscious state, with every sign of having been hysterical. Edith was lying on the slope of a small rise with her head toward the base, and her face, head and body were covered with bees that had attacked her very viciously, her face and hands were badly swollen and almost black. With much difficulty, being badly stung himself, Amos got Edith home and Dr Woolley was sent for.

Word was also sent to Edith's parents, who brought Eleanor,[95] Edith's younger sister, who was to take care of Stanley. When the doctor arrived, he at once saw that the case was a very critical

---

94 *Mount Alexander Mail*, 26th March 1901.
95 Generally known as Nell or Nellie.

73

> It will be learned with sincere regret that very little hope is entertained for the recovery of Mrs Amos Milford, of Harcourt, who was so severely stung by bees on Friday last. Brain fever has now set in, and Drs Woolley and Maxwell who are in attendance on the unfortunate lady consider there is very little prospect of her recovery.

> Mrs Amos Milford, who, as reported, was so fearfully stung by bees at her residence at Harcourt, on Friday, the 7th inst., succumbed late on Thursday night to the results of her terrible misadventure. The utmost sympathy is extended to her husband in his exceedingly sad bereavement.

one, more especially as the patient was "in a certain condition".[96] By the following Wednesday, when Edith had still not regained consciousness, the attending doctors, Dr Woolley and Dr Maxwell, diagnosed the onset of meningitis and told Amos to expect the worst.[97] Edith died late on Thursday night.[98]

Edith's funeral was held on the Saturday afternoon and a memorial service, in the Church of Christ, Harcourt, was held a week later on Sunday evening. The chapel was full when Mr. W. M'Cance preached on the text, "Some are fallen asleep." In the course of his address, the evangelist referred to Edith's quiet, consistent Christian character.[99]

Stanley was only three years old when his mother died. Grandfather George, then aged 77, must have been struck by the similarity to his own situation, his mother Mary having died at Tedburn St Mary when he was ten years old with two younger siblings. Perhaps it was as they sat under lamplight in the evening

---

96 That is to say, Edith was expecting a child.
97 *Mount Alexander Mail*, 14th April 1905.
98 *Mount Alexander Mail*, 15th April 1905.
99 *Mount Alexander Mail*, 3rd May 1905.

HARCOURT.

On Sunday evening last a memorial service was held in the Church of Christ, Harcourt, in memory of the late Mrs Amos Milford, who recently passed away under such sad circumstances. A large number assembled, the chapel being crowded, when Mr W. M'Cance preached on the text, "Some are fallen asleep." He referred to the quiet, consistent Christian character of the deceased, drawing consolation from the fact that she was simply asleep in Jesus awaiting the triumphant resurrection morn, concluding with an exhortation for all to be prepared for the inevitable end to our earthly career, which, as was the case with the departed one, may come to us without one note of warning. Miss Olive Symes beautifully sang the solo "Eternity." The chapel was nicely draped in white and the meeting was a most impressive one, and at the close there was one conversion.

Edith and Stanley.

that George recounted the events of his childhood to 28-year-old widower Amos. Whatever the circumstances, Amos learned at this time that his grandmother had been Mary Whitburn.

In due course, Amos Milford married Nell Symes, Edith's younger sister. Their first child, born 9th July 1906, was given the names Leslie Whitburn to keep alive the memory of George's long-dead mother. Two other children followed, Edith May born 25th January 1913[100] and Hazel Nellie born 24th June 1916.

Neither Amos nor Nell made any distinction between Stanley and Leslie, and the half-brothers were on good terms for the whole of their lives. A source of potential difficulty arose when the estate of James Symes (Edith and Nell's father) was distributed, because Stanley got his mother's share while Nell received the same

Amos, Leslie, Nellie and Stanley Milford.

---

100 Named after Edith May Schier (Mrs Arthur Symes).

amount, although she had three children. Aunt Eliza unfortunately mentioned this fact in front of the children, but the inequality was never allowed to become a matter of importance.

Visitors to Nell and Amos included Edith and Arthur Symes. Edith (nee Schier) was Nell's cousin (on her mother's side of the family) and Arthur was the son of Amos's first cousin Johanna Symes (nee Kimber) and Nell's first cousin Bert Symes (on her father's side of the family). This apparent tangle was not uncommon in the days of settled communities and large families. We err if we regard the Victorian and Edwardian era as being simpler times. People had to be well-versed in the complexities of relationships. You were prone to meet and transact business with people to whom you were related by blood or by marriage. Edith and Arthur were fellow members of the Church of Christ and, like Amos, Arthur conducted a large acreage of orchard.

Occasional visitors were Ruth, Jim and Muriel Hook. Auntie Ruth was Nell's sister. Jim Hook, who was about six feet six inches tall, was a Railway Stationmaster. They would come to stay for a few days each year during Jim's annual holidays. They expressed disquiet over the way in which Nell and Amos gave their children the freedom to roam about the orchard, along the water race and into the bush.[101] To Nell and Amos, however, it seemed that the Hooks were over-protective of Muriel.

Another visitor eagerly looked for, was the Afghan hawker. This bearded, turbaned man would drive his large hawker's van into the yard on his half-yearly visits, be welcomed to tea and would nurse Hazel on his knee by the fire as they yarned long into the evening.[102]

---

101 Memory of Les Milford and Hazel Normington.
102 Memory of Hazel Normington, nee Milford.

Two photos of May and Hazel.

Australian Natives Association

After the death of Ann, George Milford was only seen in public in the company of his sons. It was a routine matter to see George in Castlemaine on market day accompanied by Tom, John, Bill or Amos.[103] At George's request, Tom and Amos took George to Melbourne on one occasion. He had expressed a wish to visit the site of the Immigrant's Homes on the banks of the Yarra on St Kilda Road. When they arrived on the spot, the city had changed beyond recognition. George could not say with any accuracy where he and Ann had stayed when they arrived in January 1859.[104] Apart from these trips, George Milford was reluctant to leave the family farm in his old age.

Amos, however, was quite keen to join with other Harcourt folk on occasion. He was an active member of the Harcourt Fruit-

---

103 Memory of James D Paull, told to the author in 1967.
104 This story was told to me by Joyce Barkla, nee Woodman, granddaughter of Tom and Eliza.

growers' Association and a founding member of the Harcourt Branch of the Australian Natives Association. The ANA was quite distinct from other benefit societies with their esoteric rituals and regalia. With membership restricted to native-born Australian men, the ANA provided medical, sickness and funeral benefits while promoting national pride and setting aside time at meetings for the discussion of "national questions".[105] Soon after the formation of the Harcourt Branch in 1908, Amos became the Branch Treasurer, serving in that office till 1914. The branch was very active and held many functions. An ANA hall was built and opened in 1911 and served as the Harcourt community hall until 1991. Amos had a dry

John Milford.

---

[105] Lack, John, *Victorian Historical Journal*, Vol 89, No 2, December 2018, p. 267.

sense of humour[106] and was a regular at smoke nights and socials.

One of the first activities of the ANA branch was what might be called a "tin kettling". The *Mount Alexander Mail* of 21st October 1908 reported that Mr and Mrs John Milford, who had just returned from their honeymoon, were "serenaded" by a large number of members and friends of the Harcourt ANA minstrel troupe and orchestra on Saturday night. They were afterwards hospitably entertained by Mr and Mrs Milford and there was a program of music, speeches and a presentation of a valuable brass swinging lamp.[107]

"Hospitable entertainment" was a feature of John and Elizabeth Milford's life thereafter. It was the custom of those days for the young people of the district to gather at Lizzie and John's on a Saturday or Sunday afternoon. As the children got older, they were encouraged to bring home their friends for these weekend afternoons and Mrs. Milford's fame as a hostess became legendary.

Jack and Lizzie Milford, Bessie, Jean and Jack.

---

106 Hazel had the same sort of understated humour.
107 *Mount Alexander Mail*, Wednesday 31st October 1908.

The extended family, living in close proximity, tended to take entertainments as a family unit. There were always lots of children around. A photo surviving from this era shows Tom and Amos's families enjoying a picnic at the Harcourt reservoir on Hospital Sunday 1912, with Eliza's parents, Henry and Mary Loveland who were visiting from Bendigo. In the photo, the children are climbing all over the buggy.

Hospital Sunday, 1912.

Death of George Milford

George Milford outlived all of his Kimber in-laws and died at home at the advanced age of 86 years on 30th April 1913. He had been seen by the doctor the previous week. Cause of death was given as "old age". George was simply worn out after a lifetime of farming. His grandson Leslie remembered the occasion; Stan and Les were reluctant to go to bed because they would have to pass their grandfather lying in his coffin on the dining room table. Aunt

Eliza came to their rescue: "You don't have to be afraid of a dead body," she said.

In the custom of those days the *Mail* carried a lengthy obituary for George. However this obituary is not to be relied upon as the newspaper type-setter inadvertently re-used a block of type from the second half of the obituary of another Harcourt pioneer (Henry Ely) who had died the day before George Milford. If we were to sum up George's life we might adopt the following phrase: His industry and adaptability to the strange circumstances of the pioneering era put him on a financial footing which enabled him to be quite independent.

Picture taken about 1898. Front: George Milford, Ann, Bill, Amos. Behind: Eliza, Tom, John. Absent: Jane and Charlie.

George had made his will in 1899. The will had been written up by George's close friend Robert Goodridge of Johnston St, Castlemaine. The will carefully enumerated each parcel of land that George then owned. Each of the children was to receive a parcel of land or a monetary bequest. George had settled some land on Thomas and John during his lifetime, Bill had been well provided for by Jane and John Shilson. Amos was the residual beneficiary. The whole of George's estate was valued at £1,497/4/4 and was large enough to attract death duties.[108]

After receiving his father's bequest, Amos resolved to build a new house on the homestead block and obtained a quote from T Odgers and Co of Castlemaine for a timber house, with walls eleven feet high. It would have a nine foot verandah at the front and back with turned jarrah posts and a front door with fanlights and sidelights. Inside were mantelpieces and stove.[109] The quote, for £239, was accepted and the house was built, making it the third dwelling on the site, after the cob house of 1859 and the brick house of the late 1870s. These three homes are still standing in 2019 and a granny flat has been added at the rear of the house. With the traces of the indigenous midden, the homestead site provides a comprehensive record of long-term human occupancy.

The governor's visit

In September 1914, the annual conference of the Victorian Fruitgrowers Association was held at the ANA Hall, Harcourt. Harcourt's James Lang was the president of the association that year. During June and July, a local committee visited every householder in Harcourt to arrange accommodation for the 87 or more delegates. It was reported that only two residents had failed to take part in assisting with the conference arrangements. His Excellency Sir Arthur Stanley, Governor of Victoria, had accepted an invitation to open the conference. His Excellency would arrive on the train

---

108 Public Record Office VPRS 28/P3 Unit 368 Item 129/521, VPRS 7591/P2 Unit 494 Item 129/521.
109 T Odgers and Co, quote dated 20th January 1914.

at 10.45. After official welcomes, a banquet was to be held at 1.00 pm in Mr Seelenmeyer's newly built galvanised shed across the road from the ANA Hall. A meeting of the ladies was arranged to organise the necessary decorations. The school children were to be assembled to await His Excellency's arrival. Two months out from the actual day, anticipation was "tuned to concert pitch".[110]

On Tuesday September 15th 1914, Stanley, Leslie, Ethel, Ruby, Edgar, Irene and Bessie Milford lined up with their classmates outside the west door of the ANA Hall, waving flags to greet the Governor. The Harcourt band was in attendance, as was a large group of locals. Everyone in the crowd wore blue and white ribbons, the Governor's colours. A photographer captured the scene, the avenue of children, the youthful-looking Governor, the Premier H S W Lawson (a Castlemaine local), Mr. Lang and others. After the official opening of the conference, everyone present (including the children) adjourned for the banquet. After lunch, the official party

---

110 *Mount Alexander Mail*, 8th July 1914.

walked a hundred yards to the north where Sir Arthur planted a Bunya-Bunya. The newspaper report goes on to state: "asked to name the reserve, His Excellency did so, remarking that it was the first park to be created in the Shire of Metcalfe. It was a good thing to have plenty of parks and, although the country was open enough now, some day when Harcourt became a great city (laughter and applause) they would be thankful at having preserved spaces of land. As requested he named the reserve after himself, Stanley Park, declaring that it was earlier than he had expected his name to be immortalised (laughter and applause)".[111]

The school children were in the audience at these proceedings, and it was perhaps with some pride that Stanley and Leslie watched

> **ARBOR DAY**
>
> HARCOURT CELEBRATIONS.
>
> HONORING FALLEN SOLDIERS.
>
> A number of residents met at Stanley Park on Wednesday morning with shovels, spades, pitchforks, wheelbarrows, etc., for the purpose of digging the ground and clearing the paths. The continuous soaking rain of the past few days had saturated the ground, and places had to be reserved for laying down tile drains.
>
> In the afternoon, at three o'clock, the school children marched to the park for the purpose of celebrating Arbor Day, planting and dedicating trees and shrubs to the memory of the fallen soldiers, wounded, and returned men, but on account of inclement weather only the planting by parents and relatives of the fallen heroes was carried out.

---

111 *Mount Alexander Mail*, 16th September 1914.

as their grandfather, James Symes, posed for a photograph with Harcourt's pioneers of the 1850s. Only three of those children present in 1914 were able to be found to take part in the 75th anniversary celebrations for Stanley Park in 1989. Leslie Milford was one of the guests of honour in 1989.

In June 1918, the schoolchildren again marched to Stanley Park to celebrate Arbor Day. The event had been carefully planned and there was an immense gathering of parents and local residents. The entire Milford family would have been there, although unscathed by the war, "you went to every public event", my father told me. The Shire President and the local Methodist Minister led a ceremony of planting and dedicating trees and shrubs to the memory of Harcourt's fallen soldiers. Rain fell gently during the proceedings; the crowd watched in silence as the mothers and fathers planted the trees to memorialise five young Harcourt men who would never return from the War. The enormity of Harcourt's loss was uppermost in everyone's mind.[112]

Wartime conditions and thereafter

The orchards had yielded well for thirty years because of the abundance of water from the Malmsbury Reservoir. However, the 1915 harvest was meagre due to a dry spell at the time of fruit-set, and the export of fruit to England and Germany had ceased during the war. These two factors combined to make for a stressful time for fruit-growers across the state. A parliamentary enquiry into the industry was conducted, with the enquiry panel taking evidence at ANA Hall, Harcourt, on 19th March 1915. Evidence was given by the leading Harcourt orchardists James Lang, J H Lang, Edward

---

112 *Castlemaine Mail*, 20th June 1918.

Pritchard, Ebenezer Eagle, Luther Rash, Jacob Smith and J B Warren.

The evidence gives a good insight into orchard practices and varieties at the time. Fruit was stored in wooden kerosene or benzene boxes in a shed or under the trees for long periods, even up to October. Popular apple varieties were Jonathon, Five Crown, London Pippin, Cleopatra, Rome Beauty and Munroe's Favourite. Each orchard had about twenty percent of the area planted in pear varieties. The orchardists regularly sprayed for codling moth and thrip. Fruit sent by rail seemed to get a rough handling. Country trade was generally with retailers and greengrocers.[113]

In the meantime, the education of the Harcourt children was expanded. Leslie remembered being sent, in his later primary school years, by train to Castlemaine to attend Sloyd classes once a week, principally learning wood and metal work, at Castlemaine North Primary School. The introduction of Sloyd into the curriculum was

> **OUR EDUCATIONAL SYSTEM.**
>
> As a start in the direction of adding technical education to the curriculum of the State schools, the Public Service Board, at the request of the Education Department, is advertising for an organiser and instructor in hand and eye and manual training, with the view of introducing into our schools the Sloyd system, which has been successful in Sweden. The salary offered is L350. Two assistant instructors, at a salary of L225 each, and an instructor in kindergarten, at a salary of L210, are also wanted. The appointments are to be for three years. With the object of facilitating the appointment of these teachers, applications are being invited from persons outside as well as within the public service, it being feared that there may be no one in the Government employment at the present time qualified to impart this instruction.

113 *Victorian Parliamentary Papers 1915*, Legislative Assembly, Vol 2, pp. 273–289.

an early development in manual training and technical education. Stanley and Edgar would have attended these classes.

Advances in cool storage were also being made at this time. In January 1917, a committee was appointed by the Harcourt Fruitgrowers Association to gain information on coolstores. Their report to the March meeting was encouraging, and thirty orchardists agreed to take shares in the proposed new coolstore. Tom, John and Amos Milford were among the first to take up the £250 shares. By August of 1917, prices for coolstore machinery, building and land had been obtained, and construction proceeded with some rapidity. The coolstores opened on 1st March 1918. The stored fruit kept in good condition until the closing of the stores in November, and realised good prices.

In those days, orcharding was a cooperative effort for the Milford family. For example, spraying the fruit trees was done by a team of three brothers, with Charlie standing on the horsedrawn cart operating a hand pump, while the other two walked from tree to tree spraying up and down the branches using hoses that were being

Charlie Milford (on the dray), John (back to camera) and Amos.

fed from the pump mounted on a barrel on the cart. Pruning and picking were also labour intensive. If you were a Milford, then fruit-growing was your main pre-occupation. If you lived in Harcourt, your motto might well have been: "Nothing without labour", as it was only by hard and continuous work with brain and hand that the district attained its prestigious position as the State's foremost apple-growing district.[114]

The family orchard holdings reached their peak in the late 1920s, with a large proportion of the family's landholdings in apple and pear orchards operated by Tom, Edgar, Bill, Charlie, Amos, Stanley, Leslie and John Milford, Michael Kimber (junior) and George Cribbes (a Kimber son-in-law) on or near the block which had been first settled by Ann and George Milford on their arrival in 1859.[115]

At Devonshire Vale: 8th August 1924
All the grandchildren

The young people of the Milford family were in the habit of meeting at Bill Milford's each Friday night to play cards or draughts. Uncle Bill looked forward to these evenings and provided a supper of bread and cheese for his nephews and nieces.[116]

On this particular Friday, as they walked home from school together, thirteen-year-old Jean, her brother Jack (8), Hazel (8) and May (11) had talked about a forthcoming community celebration. Straight after tea, Bessie, aged 15, brought her sister and brother

---

114 *Mount Alexander Mail,* 15th August 1907 "Harcourt Fruit".
115 Extract from Carr, Howard 2002, *Bridging the Generations: The story of Harcourt,* p 176.
116 Devonshire tea was another favourite – bread spread with cream then with jam on top. This is true Devonshire tea, only the Cornish put the jam on the bread, then spread the cream.

Daisy Frost.

from "Brooklyn" to the back door of "Craig Elvan". This was the signal for 22-year-old Stanley, Leslie (18) and Peter Smith (also 18) to come to the door.

Peter Smith was a London orphan who had been brought to Victoria by the Victorian Police Department to be settled on a farm. Peter had been brought up in the Metropolitan and City Police Orphanage, Twickenham, as his father had been a member of the London Metropolitan Police. He had been living with Amos Milford and his family for about a year by this time, and he worked with Amos, Stanley and Leslie in the orchard.

While waiting for May and Hazel to come to the door, Daisy Frost appeared. Daisy had arrived that day with her parents. They had come down from their home at Kangaroo Flat. The entire family was to attend the big celebrations at the Harcourt Methodist

Laura.

Church on the Saturday and Sunday. Daisy, unmarried at age 36, was the oldest of the cousins. She would see all of her Frost relations at the church; she wanted to enjoy her Milford relatives tonight.

In their noisy way, the young people tramped down the lane towards "Millbrook" to round up Ethel (23) Edgar (19) and Rene (16) whom they had not seen since they had a game of kick-to-kick on the previous Saturday. The only cousins missing were Laura and Ollie.[117] Laura (expecting her first child) and her husband Robert Hallett, and her older sister Olive with her husband Bob Martin were arriving on the morrow so as to attend the church Re-Union Tea Meeting on Saturday night.[118]

Stan, Leslie, Peter and Edgar formed the advance party as

117 Their sister Ruby had died, aged 17, of the Spanish flu in 1921.
118 *Castlemaine Mail*, 9th and 12th August 1924.

the cousins climbed the hill to Uncle Bill's place. A week or two previously, the four young men had gone to a dance in Castlemaine; in the late afternoon they had travelled to the town in a buggy, their good clothes in a suitcase. They stopped at the home of Mr and Mrs Manson in Barker Street to change into their good clothes and to go on to the dance. They were looking forward to the time when Amos was to purchase a Ford car.[119] But tonight they were content to walk to Uncle Bill's.

The young men stopped briefly to watch an echidna waddling across their path. By the time the eight-year-olds arrived on the scene, the echidna had curled itself tightly into a protective ball, Jack picked up a stick with which to prod it into action, but Daisy restrained him. She had fallen into the role of carer of the youngest and the stragglers.

While the cousins were stopped, Daisy had them all look down at the scene below them. "Look at that!" she said, and, as they looked, they could see far away to the north-west, Mount Barker, then to the east Mount Alexander, illuminated by the late afternoon sunlight, while down in the valley were row upon row of trees – gum trees marking the roads, apple trees as far as the eye could see and here and there a wisp of smoke from a chimney. "Look! There's Uncle Amos's, look Jack, I can see your home!" Even the teenage girls, temporarily stayed in their chatter, started to point out the things that they could recognise. Behind them, further up the hill, Bill was standing in the doorway, a blazing open fire at his back. In front of them was the settled pattern of well-kept orchards, comfortable homesteads and roads, a wilderness that had been transformed utterly since the arrival of their grandparents sixty-five years before.

---

119 Amos purchased his first motor car, a Ford, from J R Duggan two weeks later on 25th August 1924.

We end this story, as we began, upon a high ridge. The view from Haldon Hill in South Devon, England was of extensive farmlands, owned by the lord of the manor, to which the hapless labourer would forever be tied. The view from "Mount View" in Harcourt, Victoria was of extensive orchards, vigorous and productive, owned, debt-free, by those who had worked the land from virgin bush. The Milford family had been in Harcourt for 65 years. It is appropriate to leave the children and grand-children of the pioneers at this point, with their lives, and their homesteads, stretched out before them.

Appendix One
The origin of the name Milford

Devon place names generally derive from the Saxon era. It is probable that Devon was but thinly populated when the Saxon settlers came in the seventh century of the Christian era.[120]

The Doomsday Book of 1086 lists two places named Meleforde and Melefort (modern Milford) in Devon. They were described as tiny villages with just a few houses. The names derive from the description of the locality– the fort or river ford where a melee took place.

In a small community, a surname is unnecessary. Family names came into use in England after 1066 and the Norman Conquest. We may speculate on the manner of being given a name; as a man moved his household from one village to the next, say from Melefort to another village, he may have been commonly known in his new village as William from Melefort to distinguish him from William the blacksmith. The inevitable rise in population and the increased need for official records of births, deaths and marriages helped to formalise the use of surnames.

For those interested in heraldry, during the Herald's visit to Devon in 1620 a record was made of the pedigree and armorial shield of Richard Mylford of Wickington. The shield was described as "*Argent, three oak leaves in pale all ppr.*"

---

120 Sellman, RR 1985, *Aspects of Devon History*, Devon Books, Exeter, p22.

Appendix Two
Life expectancy in rural Devon

There were twenty burials of people with the surname Milford, at Tedburn St Mary, in the forty years 1817 to 1857. Ages at death ranged from 10 weeks to 86 years. The average age at death of this small sample was 52.6 years compared to about 45 years for Great Britain as a whole. There was no discernable difference between the life expectancy of males and females. Four (20%) of the deaths were of children, compared to the national average of about twenty-five percent. While this is a small sample the fact that the life expectancy of our Tedburn kinfolk was above the national average indicates the benefit of better access to fresh produce and less exposure to infectious disease for country folk than for those living in the cities of Industrial Revolution Britain. For our ancestor George to live to 86 years was at the upper end of life expectancy.

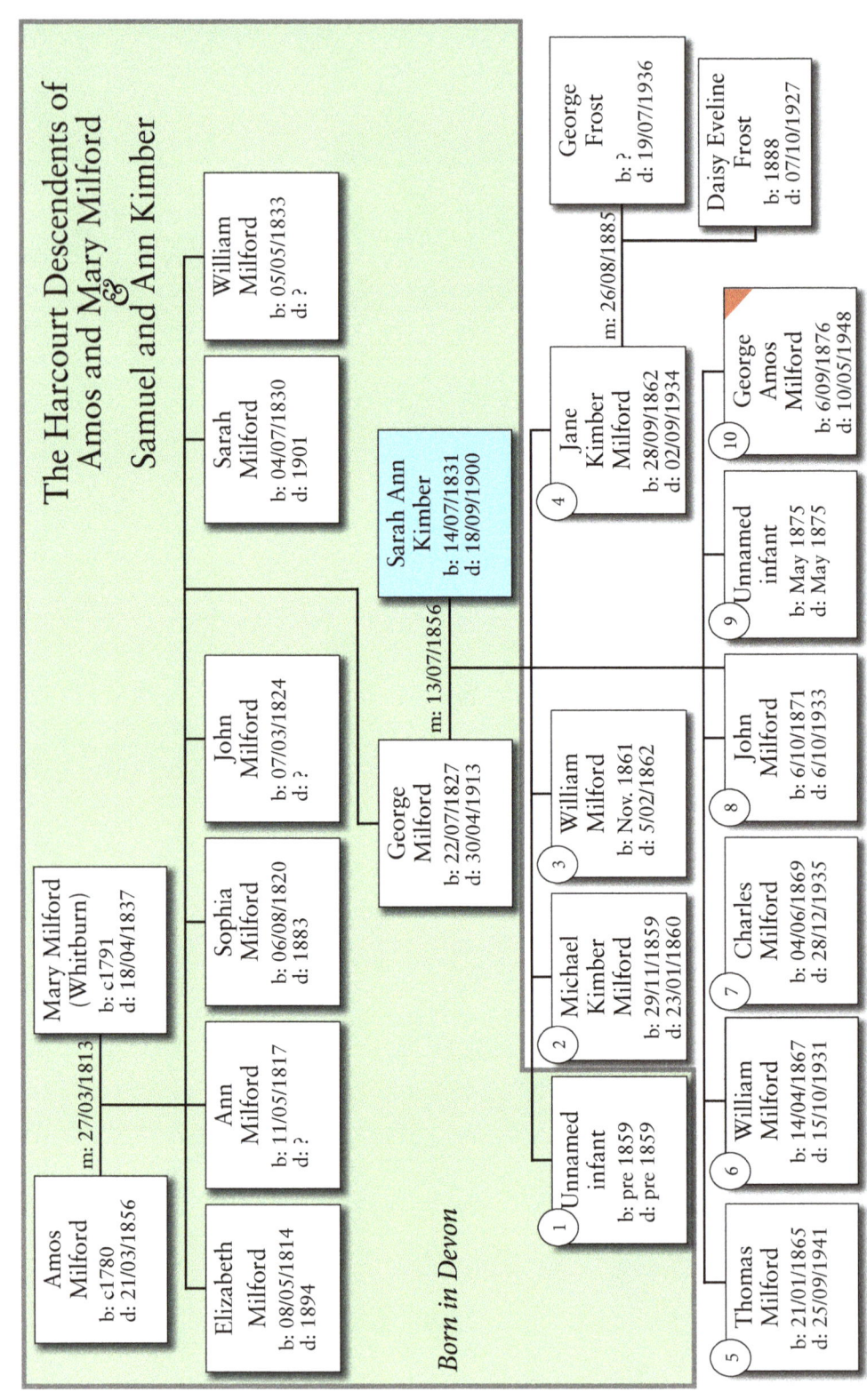

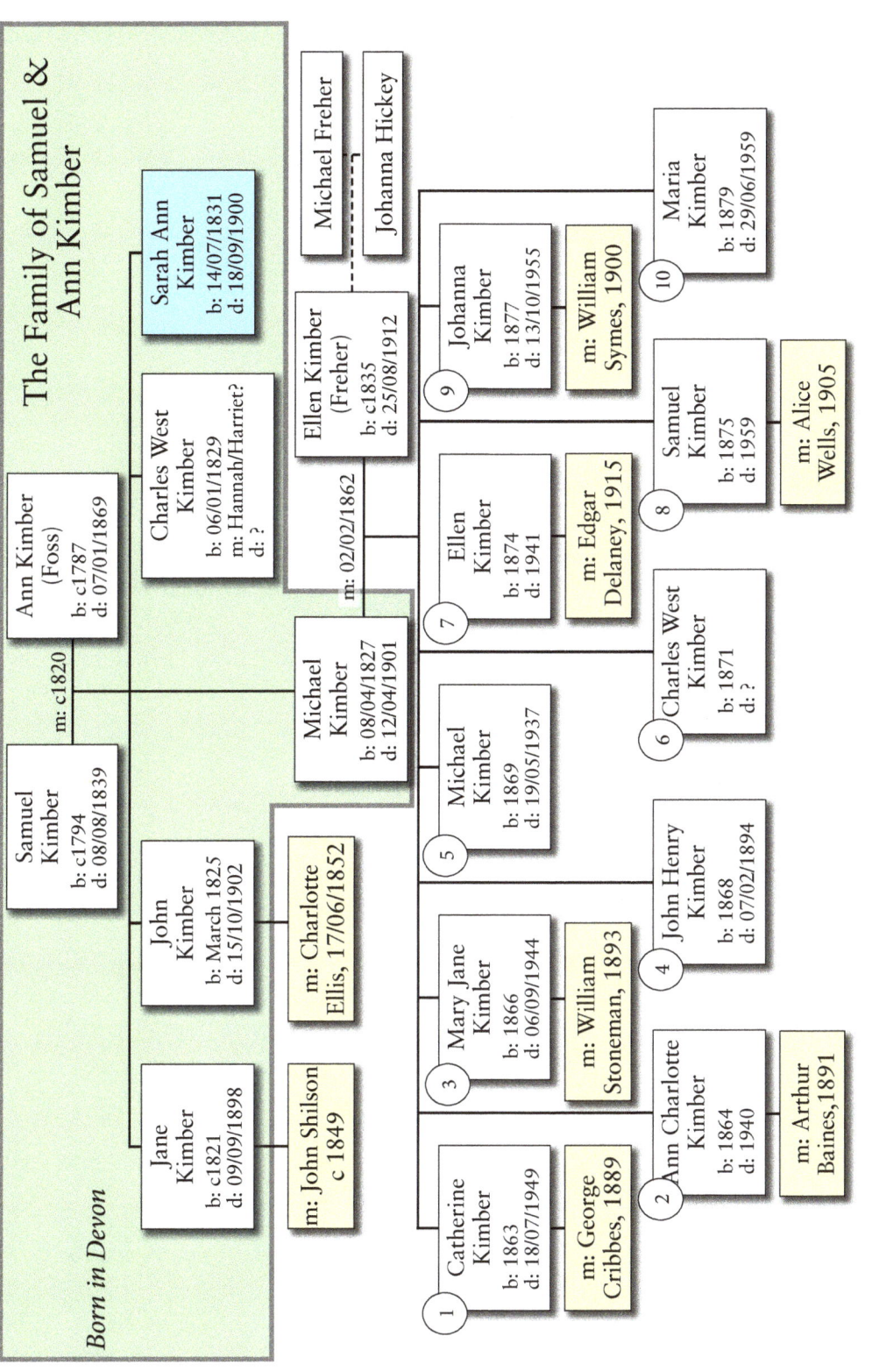

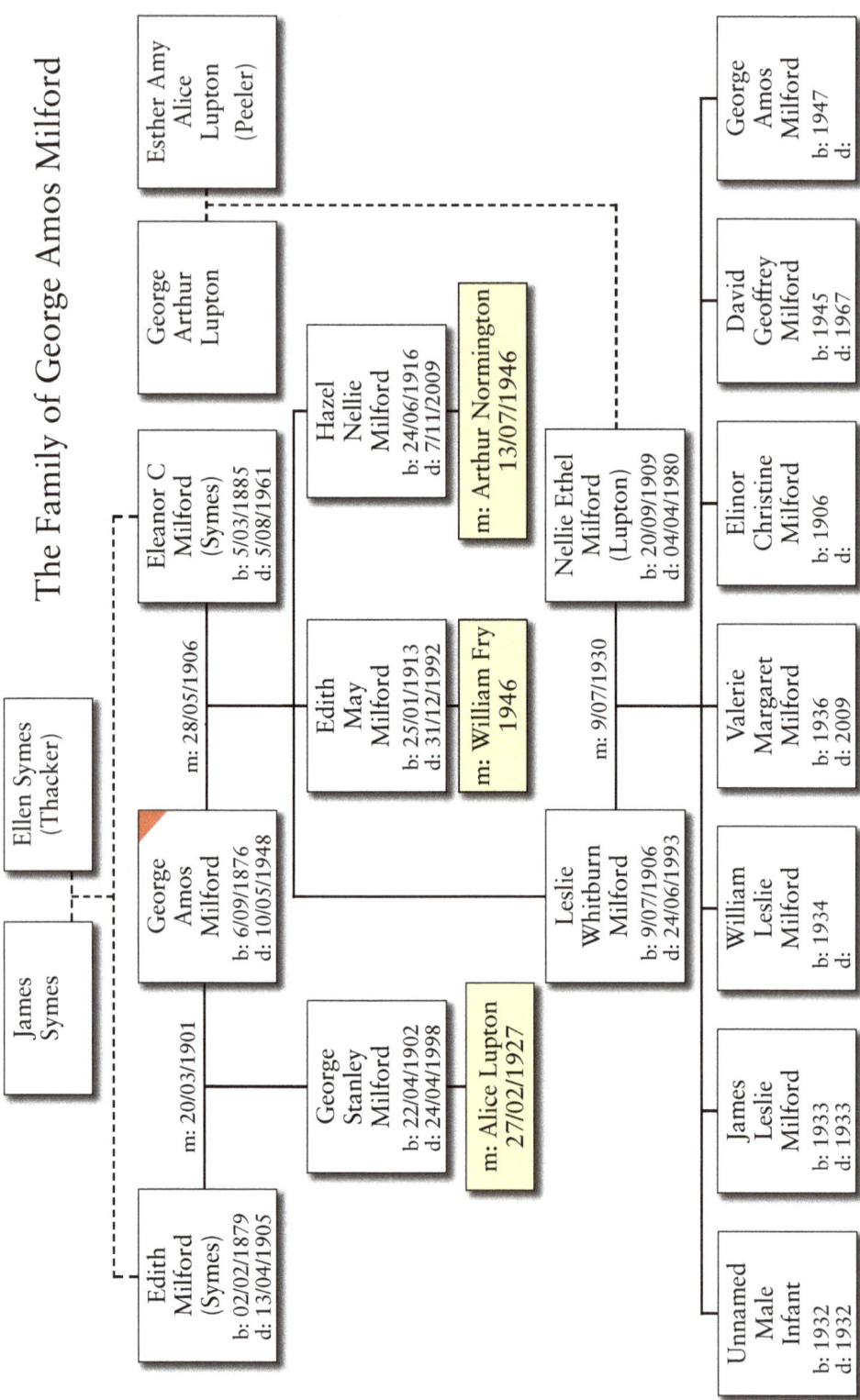

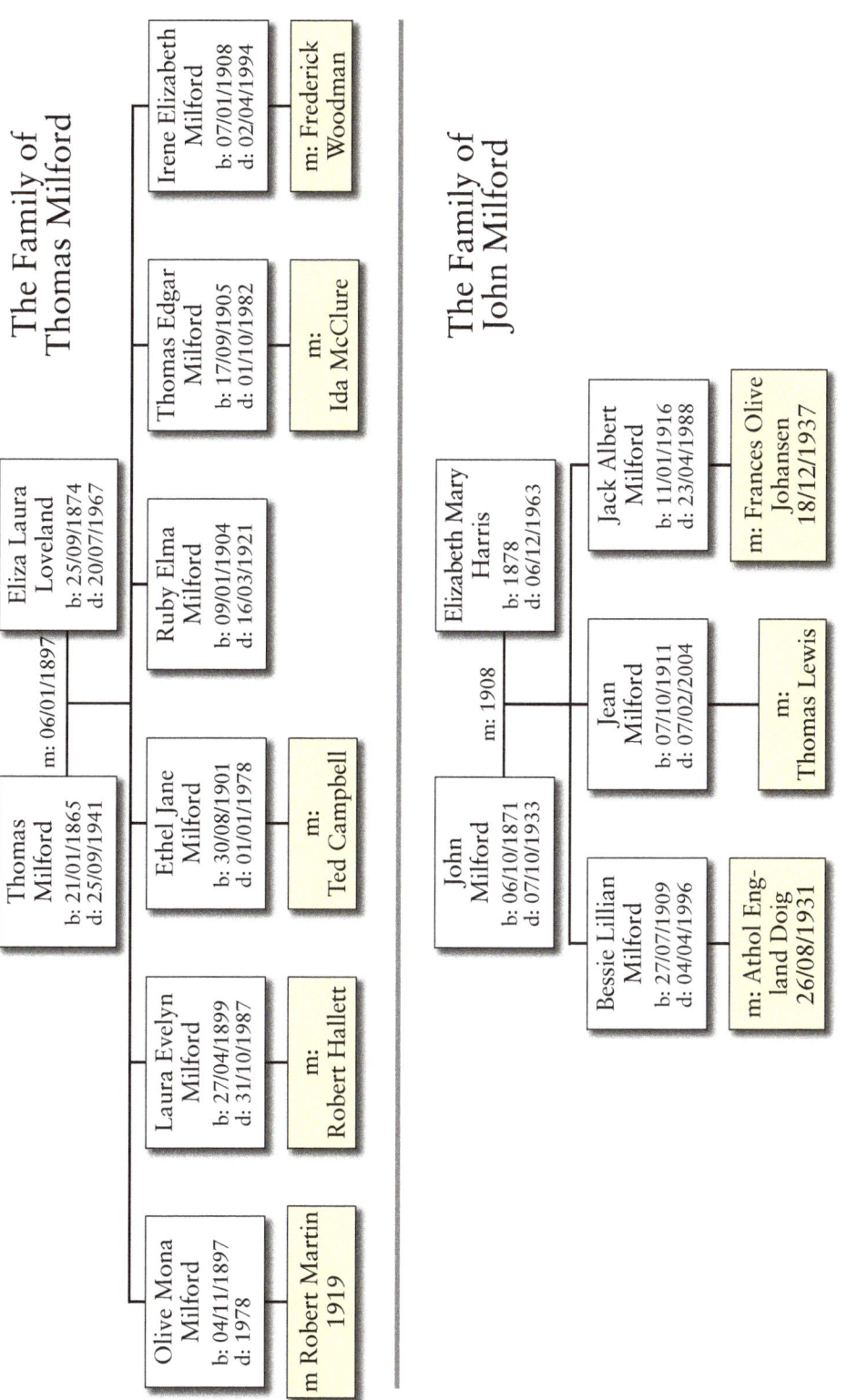

www.ingramcontent.com/pod-product-compliance
Lightning Source LLC
Chambersburg PA
CBHW062041290426
44109CB00026B/2694